The Sales Operator

Insider's Guide to Successful Selling

BRIAN J. BIELER

Author of *Powerful Steps* and *Rich and Free*

Also By
Brian J. Bieler

Powerful Steps—10 Essential Career Skills and Business Strategies for the Workplace Warrior

Rich and Free—The Entrepreneur's Guide to Creating Wealth and Personal Freedom

The Sales Operator
Insider's Guide to Successful Selling

Copyright © 2008 by Brian J. Bieler

Published By:
Little Falls Press
7000 North 16th Street, Suite 120 # 489
Phoenix, AZ 85020-5547

1-800-980-5099

powerfulsteps@cox.net

Visit our website:
www.powerfulsteps.com

Unattributed quotations are by Brian J. Bieler

ISBN-10: 0-9779569-4-6
ISBN-13: 978-0-9779569-4-4

Edited By Sandford Tuey

Cover design by

Blue Bus Media
Los Angeles, CA 310-985-5165
www.bluebusmedia.com

To Ann

*Who has inspired me and shared
all the best years of my life*

People come into sales with the expectation that the game is easy and anyone can sell. Many expect companies and products to do the heavy lifting. That is not how it works. Great salesmanship comes from competence. There is no simple formula or tried-and-true method for sales success.

The way to stay ahead of the sales game is to become a non-stop learner. While selling does not require a degree, it does require education. Go get the skills and knowledge you need. Develop a winning edge by exploiting your individual talents.

Thank you for being my customer and buying this book. I hope you enjoy it. My goal is to provide you with a resource so helpful that you will not hesitate to refer it to friends and colleagues.

Please visit our website at **www.powerfulsteps.com** and send me a note. Let me know how you're doing in your career and how my book has helped.

To The Most Important Skill In Business

Sales

Table Of Contents

Introduction

I have years of valuable experience and knowledge to share with you. It's real-life lessons I learned while selling and running companies. Since the mid 1990's we have witnessed unprecedented change in our living standards and economy.

The internet has reinvented the way we share knowledge and information and while it seems we have come a long way in a short time, we are only at the beginning of a powerful global conversion.

Markets and consumers get smarter. Companies scramble to keep up as people share information worldwide. New technologies invite competitors to leapfrog old ways of doing business.

In previous generations, it took tycoons decades to create fortunes with hard assets and real estate. Today millionaires are created in the blink of an eye taking advantage of speed in changing technologies.

This new kind of competition has little boundaries. Knowledge and information, once rare, secretive and expensive, have become common commodities.

Years of technical advances ramp up sharp productivity gains. We crank out stuff so fast it's unimaginable how we did things in the past. The tables have turned. We have shifted from a seller's economy to a buyer's and consumer's economy. New economic times have changed sales philosophy as buyers and consumers are in the power position.

In years of high demand, sellers are in control and buyers pay up. More goods and services in the marketplace change things fast.

Even as the population grows and markets expand, productivity and innovation have pushed supply ahead of demand. Salespeople front and center on the firing line are witnessing this first hand.

In previous generations, salespeople had the upper hand because product shortage created sales tactics and strategies to take advantage of the times. With less competition, it was easier to raise and control prices. In the past, few sellers needed negotiating skills. *Learning strong closing tactics was far more important than personal skills and product knowledge.*

New Times for Sellers

Salespeople need to sharpen skills. It's a new game. As buyers and consumers deal with more choices, buying decisions become more confusing. Once easy to make choices are now confusing decisions. As we deal with endless varieties of goods and services, who is to know the best choice? How do we know one product or service from another?

In the past, we had three TV network channels and limited programming. Now we have cable and satellite delivering hundreds of channels and an avalanche of programming. Why then do people complain there is nothing to watch on television? The answer is too many choices.

At one time, we had three dominant car manufacturers and a dozen or so top cars to choose from. Now we have hundreds of cars in every size and type. It goes on from food, furniture, travel, restaurants, movies, clothes and you name it. We have more options and more opportunity.

Salespeople are selling in new times. Sellers who don't upgrade skills, strategies and tactics to match the thinking and economy will find a savvy consumer and a younger generation that has a very different mindset than past generations. Few today will respond to arm twisting hard closing tactics and old school sound bites. The old sales strategies of a high demand economy are over.

Sellers focused on help, support and service with strong personal skills will be in high demand.

Two Views

I wrote this book from seller's and manager's experience so you can see both sides of the sales picture. It's an insider's view of what it takes to be a success in today's sales environment.

The book is in two parts. Part I is about critical personal skills. Sellers must develop themselves to reach full potential. Selling is a professional trade and demands peak performance to earn the rewards. To reach full potential, you must first improve yourself and your skills. The personal skills and assets you develop are yours for life and go with you wherever you go.

Part II of the book is about essential sales skills. Being brilliant at basics and fundamentals is paramount in the age of knowledge and information. Today, salespeople deal with smarter enlightened buyers and customers. They must be up to the task with the latest skills and product knowledge or people will not trust them to help them make buying decisions.

Professional athletes and the successful do not stop learning because they reach a higher level of success. They hire coaches, find mentors and become the masters of their trade. In order for sellers to turn professional, they need to act like professionals and not simply employees.

Relationship selling will become even more important because of increased competition. Customers consider relationships as important as or more important than the product or service.

The product you sell is likely available from someone else. Customers can buy from you or not at all. People buy from you because they trust you and believe what you say is true. People buy from you because they trust you more than they trust your competitor.

The secrets of motivation, the most misunderstood skill and negotiation, the least respected skill, are in this book. Tips and ideas on better communication, the absolute must have skill, are in the chapters ahead.

You can never learn enough as you work your way up the sales ladder. No one has all the answers. It takes skills, knowledge and a sense of humility to deal with important decision makers. To land the big fish and important sales, you must work your way up to a higher level of business expertise.

Chinese warrior Sun Tzu taught us to win the battle in the mind before the fight. Winning means being prepared. Selling is one thing but making big money in sales will tax your abilities and make you work smart and strategically.

Enjoy this book. Use a magic marker, highlight ideas, dog-ear the pages. It's a resource guide designed to add to your unique talents, strengths and abilities.

I wish you good selling and have fun. The future for professional salespeople has never been brighter.

PART I

Your Personal Skills Define You

Top performing salespeople are different ages, sexes and come from different backgrounds. They have different styles and different goals. What they have in common is they *don't follow conventional thinking.*

People rarely get to the top on job skills alone. It takes more to be a winner than simply doing a job well. Yet many take for granted the very things that make them big winners, their personal development.

Experience tells us 80 percent of salespeople focus on job skills alone and this is a critical reason they stay average. The top performing 20 percent of sellers master personal skills or the "soft stuff" and that's why they get ahead. Communication skills are more than charisma; they are the must-have skills of world-class sellers.

Without strong personal skills, you may wind up a commodity. If you open your mouth and find you are blistering paint, selling may not be the best choice of occupation. If your idea of selling is hierarchical power and strong-arm tactics that went out with the last generation of thinking.

> *Developing excellent communication skills is absolutely essential to effective leadership. The leader must be able to share knowledge and ideas to transmit a sense of urgency and enthusiasm to others. If a leader can't get a message across clearly and motivate others to act on it, then having a message doesn't even matter.*
>
> **—Gilbert Amelio**
> Former President and CEO
> National Semiconductor Corporation

The chapters in Part 1 are strategies and ideas that give you a critical edge and make the difference in a career. Master these skills and you will be on your way to top performance selling.

CHAPTER 1

Attitude Starts Here

Your attitude doesn't only affect you, it affects everything around you. Attitude lends integrity and implies people can trust the value of what you are selling.

I learned how to sell with a garden-variety tool: enthusiasm. In the beginning, my positive attitude, commitment and persistence made up for my youth and inexperience. I was far too young to make distinctions about what I was doing. What I did understand was a positive attitude helped me sell and that kept me motivated.

If you are persistent enough, something will happen; it always does. Staying the course determines the outcome, not how long it takes. Persist long enough and you win. Develop a thick skin and don't let negative people influence your thinking. Keep your attitude positive.

It's How We React

Success comes from behavior; it's what we do that counts. However, selling is spontaneously unpredictable and filled with surprises at every turn. More often than not, our success is how we think on our feet and how we react to things that happen to us.

Selling success does not come to us in a nice straight upward line. Adjusting to new surroundings and changing environments is what makes us winners. How we think creates our success.

The power of positive thinking is more than metaphysical. Our thinking creates a blueprint and guide for successful selling strategies; *our thinking leads us to action.*

Making Mistakes And Learning More

Thomas Edison made 1,000 mistakes before he discovered how to make a light bulb work. Making mistakes is a precursor to success. You cannot sell and influence others if you do not try. You learn from your mistakes. Top sales performers win because they *don't stop trying.*

The more mistakes you make, the faster you figure out the right things to do. Mistakes are **learning experiences** and a key part of winning.

The batting average of .300 in baseball is considered good; an average over .400 is nearly an unachievable goal. The last player that did it was Ted Williams of the Boston Red Sox in 1941 who hit a .406. The average batter is not hitting 70% of the time! Anyone who thinks they come close to 100% perfection in the sales game is kidding themselves.

No Free Lunch

Expect good things to happen. However, it's naïve and unprofessional not to be prepared for the worst. When you prepare for the worst, it is never as bad as it could have been.

You can have almost anything you want as long as you are willing to go for it. Successful sellers have the right attitude but accept the fact that selling is not a bed of roses. Winners wear seat belts and that is why they survive crashes. Success has little to do with being fair or equitable. Build yourself up and push yourself to gain strength. You must have the mental muscle to stay in the game.

Develop spine and become self-reliant or you will quit at the first signs of rejection or tough times. Obstacles are not a statement of fact. Obstacles are something you figure out how to get around.

Whether you're new to sales or an old pro, it matters little. It's your attitude about what you're doing to earn your living. What are you willing to do to achieve your personal goals? How many "Nos" are you willing to take before you get to the "Yes" you need? Are you willing to change what you are today to get what you want tomorrow?

Without Persistence
Commitment Means Little

Desire to be successful must be strong. If you are not persistent, you need to develop that strength and attitude. Selling is a game of curve balls continually thrown at you. That's why it's so important to let adversity bounce off you and keep on going like the Energizer Bunny.

Selling Is Marathon, Not A Sprint

Prepare yourself to stay in the race until you cross the finish line. A defined time frame is not as important as your ability to keep running at the goal. Develop strong desire and commitment. Above all, be persistent.

> *This is the lesson: never give in, never give in, never, never, never, never—in nothing, great or small, large or petty—never give in except to convictions of honour and good sense. Never yield to force; never yield to the apparently overwhelming might of the enemy.*
>
> **—Winston Churchill**

Attitude Sets Up Opportunity

Your positive attitude sets you up but attitude alone is not enough in sales to get you to the head of the class.

Selling is little different from professional investing, management or learning how to be a doctor. To earn more money and improve your career you must **learn the skills of the trade.**

When I started selling radio advertising in Miami, I had six years of experience behind me. My sales were ahead of budget but I know there was business I was missing. I was dealing in an old boys' network of advertisers and had little advantage.

"Why can't I do more?" I kept asking myself and finally it came to me. The professional media buyers that were the majority of my sales potential had me at a disadvantage. They had knowledge and skills I did not understand. They had the upper hand.

Norman was my boss and one of the few people in Miami at the time who had national media research experience and a statistical background. His last job had been creating national sales presentations for radio and TV broadcasters. Norman's experience was unique and I saw the opportunity.

Norman came to the offices early so I joined him when no one was around and the office was quiet. I badgered him to teach me the technical side of media advertising. I knew how things worked; I wanted to learn why things happened. Radio ratings and numbers would be sales ammunition if I could use them to show advertisers how to sell more products.

Being a slow learner it took me forever to learn this new math and way of thinking. Finally, I understood enough to change my way of selling. I moved from selling advertising to helping people figure out how to be better marketers and advertisers so they could sell more products.

It didn't take long for my ideas to start working and my sales increased dramatically. I was consulting as much as I was selling. At that point, people began to see me as a professional and they trusted me. I became a valued resource and that changed everything.

My attitude drove me to learn more. Paranoia and fear of failing was my motivation. Coming from a family of salespeople and entrepreneurs, instinctually I knew:

It's Not Your Bosses' Job To Make You A Sales Success, It's Their Job To Give You Tools And Training To Become Successful

My success became who I knew. I met more people because it was easy to get introductions and referrals from my accounts. The unique knowledge I gained led me to better relationships with customers. The more value I added, the more my sales increased.

I was winning the sales game with attitude and persistence. However, attitude has limitations. I could see clearly after my experience that attitude set me up for success but attitude alone was not enough.

It was not until I sharpened my skills *combined* with my positive attitude that my career took on a new dimension.

Attitude and commitment are critically important because it helps keep you in the sales game. However, skills and education separate you from average. If you stay in the sales game long enough, you gain time to improve your skills. You must be proactive about staying on the leading edge and continuing your education. Your knowledge must be current and your skills up to par to win in today's competitive environment.

Selling Is Not An Either/Or Proposition. You Need Skills, Knowledge *And* A Positive Attitude.

Selling is performance and skill based. Sales jobs turn over quickly. Pressure is on sellers to sell and close sales. Trying to break into sales is a Catch-22. Many new to selling find it tough and are washed out before they learn the insider's skills. What keeps people in the sales game is attitude and enthusiasm.

Head Games

Be cautious of workshops and books simply built on PMA, positive mental attitude. Telling people attitude alone makes you a winner is easy to write about and takes little real experience to talk about. That was old school thinking and is generations behind. It's not enough to get people excited and energized. Attitude works when it leads you to action.

Attitude without action, strategy, knowledge and skills will mean little beyond getting you to average performance. The insider's secret is, it takes **brains, skills and attitude to create success:**

> *Press on: nothing in the world can take the place of perseverance. Talent will not; nothing is more common than unsuccessful men with talent. Genius will not; un-rewarded genius is almost a proverb. Education will not; the world is full of educated derelicts. Persistence and determination alone are omnipotent.*
>
> **—Calvin Coolidge**
> 30th President United States

Push yourself to learn the specialized skills of your trade, become brilliant at the basics and your positive attitude will push you as far as you want to go.

Selling is entrepreneurial. If you start with confidence and the right attitude, you can sell and improve your skills.

However, many are not prepared for the challenges of selling. They think it's a "piece of cake" and easy to accomplish. What a surprise the sales game is to the unprepared!

If your sales results are not what you would like them to be, consider training and acquiring new skills. Investing in professional sales training is a proven way to help sellers.

Attitude, commitment and persistence are the critical ingredients like the spark plug in an engine. However, to be a top performing seller your skills must match your mindset.

The winning combination to improving sales is learning new skills, acquiring knowledge and keeping a positive can do attitude.

How You
Think Is Everything

- Selling Demands A Thick Skin – The Strong Survive

- Attitude Keeps You In The Sales Game

- Sales Success Takes Time, Persistence And Courage

- Don't Wait Around For Help To Come To You, Go Get What You Need

- Mistakes Are Nothing More Than Learning Experiences On The Way To Winning

CHAPTER 2

Communication Strategies Of Today's Sales Professional

Have you noticed that people have answers to your thoughts before you finish a sentence? People are so anxious to make points they don't even wait for you to catch your breath before they have your answer.

The average person speaks at 125 to 150 words a minute. That's slow motion for our minds. We have a mental capacity to understand 400 words a minute. We get bored easily when others speak.

To compound the problem, over 40 percent of the words used in spoken language are non-essential. It's easy to get the message of others without all the words. Our minds are like powerful car engines idling while waiting for the green light to signal interesting or essential information coming.

Unless speakers deliver a dynamic presentation or unless we are extremely interested in the subject, our minds juggle a lot of other information while we are supposedly paying attention.

Thinking about making sales points at the expense of what a prospect is actually telling us leads to misunderstandings and lost sales.

We have formal training in speaking, reading and writing but little guidance how to listen. We need only bits and pieces of information to set off our natural tendency to form opinions and make judgments. We are so smart we often outsmart ourselves. It's an epidemic problem in business. People are lousy listeners.

Thinking ahead in conversations is no sign of intelligence. In sales, it's often a sign of arrogance and belligerence. In our professional lives, it's the equivalent of foot in mouth disease. You would think people get paid commissions on how many words fly out of their mouths.

Listening Is Hard Work

The average person remembers only 50 percent of what is said. No matter how intensely we attempt to absorb information, it's no easy trick to remember what people tell us.

The Challenge Is
Not To Construct Ideas
And Responses
While Others Speak

Listening ahead of conversations may be subconscious or it may be on purpose. Either way, nothing will kill a sale faster than having others think you have no interest in understanding them.

The secret to active listening is to relax. Absorb information without responding quickly. Build listening habits into a sales skill.

Selling is communicating, persuading *and* getting people to act on your ideas. You cannot sell others if you do not understand them; all you can do is talk *at* them. That is why it is far more important to be a good listener than simply being able to speak well.

Closing Sales Needs Only A Few Well-Chosen Words If You Know What Others Want

Seven percent of communication is verbal. Thirty five percent of communication is tone and emotion, the rest is body language. It's obvious what's not spoken in words is said in emotions. You will not understand others fully by simply listening. You must watch body language and hear emotions. If you do not pay attention, important things signaled to you may go right over your head.

People speak but convey meaning in emotions and body language. What is behind the words is the real message and meaning.

It's Never the Story, It's Always the Emotion

People give us feedback with folded arms, laughter, grins, pacing around, growling or raising their eyebrows. Their emotions show us how they feel if we are looking. People say one thing verbally but may be emotionally saying something else.

You learn interests of others when you are an active listener. Active listening is more than simply listening to the spoken word. When you understand how people feel, you have honest, authentic communication.

Active listeners don't judge or form opinions before they understand what others are saying. They focus on learning what is on the other person's mind.

Paradigms And Pigs

Joel Barker popularized the concept of paradigm shifts for the corporate world. His book *Future Edge* published in 1992 was listed as one of the most influential books of the time. We told paradigm stories in our sales meetings:

A sales executive was driving a Porsche Cabriolet. She had special ordered the new car delivery at the factory in Germany. She wanted to drive her car in Europe while on vacation. Heading south to the French countryside, she found herself in the mountains on a winding narrow road. There was barely enough room for two cars to pass each other.

The sun was out, the top was down and mechanical music was coming from the engine. A short straightaway appeared and with no one else on the road, she floored it. The car lunged ahead and felt like the front wheels would lift off the ground. Suddenly, around a corner just ahead of her an old pick up truck appeared weaving side to side almost out of control. She cut the wheel and swerved onto the shoulder of the road to avoid an accident.

As the man in the truck drove by he yelled out his window, "Pig, Pig" with a heavy French accent.

She yelled back as loud as she could, "You're a jerk" feeling content she insulted the driver. These French people are lousy drivers she thought, no manners and driving all over the road.

The nerve of that guy calling *me* a pig!

She downshifted gears, floored the gas to power drift through a turn and crashed into a huge pig standing in the middle of the road.

Whether you are new to sales or a veteran at this business, a seller's job is to LISTEN.

How To Improve Sales Listening Skills:

1. **Listen ahead of conversations correctly.** Don't behave like a coiled spring ready to answer questions or problems. Never interrupt while others are talking, wait for others to complete their thoughts. Learn how to relax and take in information.

2. **Reaffirm what you hear and validate what you learn.** It makes people more comfortable when you are not trying to outfox or out think them with quick answers. It also gives you time to absorb information and THINK.

3. **Do not be quick to judge or form opinions.** The job of sellers is to understand and help others and make a living from them, not judge them.

4. **Use your eyes.** Look at who you are talking to, watch their eyes and pay attention to their body communication and emotions in what they say. If you do not watch, you do not learn.

5.   **Practice.** Rehearse how you will respond in sales situations.

Happy Drugs

Stories told by people about themselves, their jobs, lives and interests are important. Pay attention and listen to people not only to sell them, but also to show interest in them personally. The more interested you are in others, the more charming you become. It becomes physical.

To Be An Interesting Person, *Be Interested*

Everyone has heard about the "runner high" or euphoria from exercising aerobically. Something physically happens in your body when you jog, run or exercise hard enough. Exercise triggers the releases of endorphins and that enhances the mood and makes you feel good.

When you listen to others and hang on their words, watch their body movements for approval, you make them feel good about themselves. That also helps release endorphins. When people feel good about others they are speaking with, it enables real authentic conversations. The more you acknowledge others, the more charming you become, the more interesting you are, the more people gravitate to you and feel good about themselves.

Yes, Repeat That

Nothing confirms understating better than feedback. Be like a parrot, echo back in different words. It assures people you understand.

Showing interest is not difficult. Be sincere. Don't zero in on every word to find sales points but do ask open-ended questions. If you put a question to someone that only requires a yes or no answer, you may get a closed yes or no response. You are a seller; you want more communication, not less. To learn more, ask questions that start with:

Who, How, When, Where, Which, What, Why

Opened ended questions cause people to answer with open-ended answers. This allows you to ask more questions.

To project your ideas, you will need enough natural emotion and conviction that others may see. Show passion and enthusiasm. When energy levels are low, you cannot project excitement and a sense of urgency.

Communication Strategies To Help You Sell And Persuade Professionally:

1. **Use All of You.** Your body is your overwhelming feature. Use all your personal impact to make your points. Eye contact, facial expressions, body and posture say more with fewer words.

2. **Find Common Ground.** Active listeners plan a response *after* others finish speaking. Position the conversation to a middle or common

ground. That enables you to sell ideas from the same viewpoint or perspective of others.

3. **Acknowledge What Others Say.** Nothing is more important to others than being understood. When people speak, show interest and respond; *you are enhancing your own position.*

4. **Respect Different Viewpoints.** Do not listen just to support your sales ideas or points of view. Don't try to make others conform to all of your ideas or they may reject your sales points even if it's in their best interest.

5. **Stay On The Topic.** Don't change the subject in mid-stream. Wait for others to complete the thought or it may come across as, "I don't care what you just said."

6. **Raise The Gradient Slowly.** If you put a frog in a pot of hot boiling water, it will jump out. If you put a frog in a pot of cool water and slowly turn up the heat, the frog will slowly get accustomed to the temperature rising. The frog never feels the heat rising. That heat rising is the *gradient.* Slowly raise intensity of powerful sales ideas *or people will jump out of the pot* before you complete your sales points.

7. **Never Talk In Absolutes.** You never *know* what others are thinking; you can only *assume* what they are thinking. Do not start thoughts with definitive answers to make sales points.

8. **Resolve Differences.** Belligerence is a bad tactic for salespeople. Don't compromise others to make sales points.

9. **Keep Your Ego In Check.** Show humility, affinity and compassion. The stronger your sales position, the more careful you have to watch your speech and behavior.

Humor Helps Build Rapport

One of the lessons not taught in college is to get along with others, smile, be yourself and have a sense of humor. Humor is the key element in politics, leadership and a strategic tool of professional sellers.

President Lincoln had a repertoire of homespun stories and President Reagan sold his ideas and made points with one-liners.

Salespeople who joke, make fun of situations and poke fun at themselves, make people smile and laugh. You do not have to be a comedian to have a sense of humor. However, without humor and a lighter side it is hard to show humility and affinity.

People will have a hard time warming up to you if you are stiff as a board. Make people smile and feel comfortable to be around you, it will open up conversation and feelings. It's a great start to building relationships and makes you a better communicator. A sense of humor is an indispensable sales tool.

Get Focused

We deal with distractions, it's part of the sales job description. In a fast-paced business world, communication skills have focused on hand-held text messaging devices, email, computers and cell phones. It has led to poor speaking and listening habits in our jobs and in our personal lives.

Say what you mean. Time is short. Be a good communicator and get to the point quickly with a complete message or you may lose people's attention.

It's hard to get people excited about data and information. Sellers must be able to communicate more than literal laundry lists of features and benefits. People listen to ideas and buy concepts.

The Master Communicator Influences Others

You cannot determine needs without knowing what people want. That is why of all the personal skills, communication is the most important.

People will forget PowerPoint presentations, slide shows, information, data and all the logic you can give them. You will be extremely lucky if they remember even half of what you present. However, people never forget how you made them feel. People buy from people they value, trust and *people they like!*

Sellers communicate ideas and influence others. While communication and speaking skills are important for business executives, they are not just an option for salespeople. Sellers must have strong communication skills to reach their full potential.

Develop an attitude of service in your sales communication. Serving others *is your job*. Let people know you are there to help them make good decisions. If you can get that communication across, you can be successful.

How You
Think is Everything

- Your Ears Earn You A Living
- Understanding Others Helps You Sell Yourself And Your Ideas
- Develop An Attitude Of Service
- Don't Listen Ahead Of Conversations
- Relax And Listen, Take In Information
- Ask Open Ended Questions
- Acknowledge What Others Say
- Make Others Feel Good About Themselves And They Will Feel Good About You
- Humor Builds Rapport

CHAPTER 3

It's About Relationships

Have you gone shopping for a car and come back with more to say about the salespeople than you did about the car you were supposed to be buying? Was it an experience you would wish on people you really detest?

Richard Dreyfuss and Danny DeVito starred in a movie about aluminum siding salesman. The setting was Baltimore in the 1950's. The movie was voted one of the best contributions to sales scams of the century.

Aluminum siding salespeople promised homeowners commissions or referral fees for neighbors who bought siding from them. They even told homeowners the siding would be free and they would have to pay only for labor.

It was a scam. In the end, customers wound up paying more for work they had been led to believe would cost less.

The movie got plenty of attention. It was close enough to reality to be a wake-up call for consumers. It made sleazy hard-closing sales strategies well known. People began naming over-the-top arm twisting salespeople after the movie, "Tin Men."

Muscling Customers

Strong-arm sales strategies in car sales, aluminum siding and insurance were widespread and helped give sellers everywhere a black eye.

Plaid suits and hard sell tactics defined selling for generations. Much of the thinking came from industrial age companies. Salespeople were not thinking up sales strategies on their own. Ideas were crafted from top marketing and sales executives.

Hard closing sales strategies were an integral part of the hierarchal business philosophy. It was accepted behavior that sales success came first and customers came second. After all, "It's only business."

Dale Carnegie published *How to Win Friends and Influence People* in 1936. The book is still on bestseller lists today. Dale told us the importance of relationship selling some 80 years ago. Relationships have been the key reason for sales success year after year.

In the industrial age, few people had access to backroom knowledge how sales strategies were created. The average middle class consumer was naïve to business practices and many behaved like sheep being fleeced.

What Changed?

Halfway through the 20th century, new technologies emerged. The internet, computers and communications changed the face of business. By the end of the 20th century, information had become virtually free. If you wanted information about products, you could now find out the good and the bad.

As consumers became enlightened, sellers could no longer assume average people have fallen off the back of a turnip truck and you could sell them anything. In the information age, it's better to assume people are perceptive and likely to know seventy-five percent as much as you about the product you are selling.

People who do not know as much as sellers at the beginning of a sale or relationship may take a tour on the internet and catch up to competitive knowledge quickly. Access to knowledge and information has changed sales strategies.

Change Reprograms Buying Habits

The more things change, the more we adjust. Change has not made us less optimistic, but as a society, we are more realistic.

People have the same wants and needs. Human nature and business have not changed. People *change buying habits and how they do things*. Change comes faster in a competitive marketplace. Along with new technology, people are usually ahead of the lag time in government and business thinking. Consumers are on the front line. Politicians and companies are often the last to figure out what is changing in the marketplace.

Why Not?

Unless people are socially, financially or materially tied to a way of doing things they have little trouble changing attitudes and buying habits. Most people quickly accept new ideas and many times are ahead of what researchers and companies are thinking. People have incentive to do what works, buy what adds value and is cost efficient.

Better products and ideas win people over quickly in all demographics. The young change fast, but thinking that older people resist change is a myth. Seniors are leading change agents and mentally years younger than previous generations.

Companies try to hold on to what is working as long as they can, but innovation and technology force change or they run the risk of losing to competition.

Economists tell us in headline news what many are already experiencing or have figured out. It's a new paradigm for sellers, marketers and advertisers.

No, They Don't

People don't have to buy from you; they may buy from your competitor or they may not buy at all. In a competitive market, your product may be available somewhere else and possibly at a better price or value.

The more competitive the market place, the more important relationships become. This has given new meaning to the sales adage: It's not what you know, *it's who you know.*

The Equalizer

People buy from you because of profoundly simple principles:

People Buy From You Because:

1. They Like You

2. They Trust You

3. Believe What You Say Is True

Relationships are the great equalizer for sellers and it drives competitors nuts. New products, services and the internet create more choices. More choices make buying decisions difficult. As technology and productivity improve, it tips the balance of supply and demand. As supply outstrips demand, sales relationships become more important and change the selling environment.

Trust in sellers helps buyers make distinctions about products. The more competition, advertising, marketing and confusion, the more important sales relationships become.

Customer-Base Relationships Selling

Relationship selling is based on customer's wants. This style of selling applies to almost any kind of business, product or service. What changes is the sales process depending on the business style or type. However, the concept of building relationships is consistent: relationship selling is consultative problem solving.

Focus On Customers Needs

1. The better your product or service fits your customer's needs, the more sales you will be able to create. Ask questions and be sure you can identity what your customer needs or wants.

2. Customers are sales perceptive, they can spot insincere sellers and may be turned off before a sale or relationships can even get started.

3. When customers know you sincerely care about what they want and need, they feel more secure buying from you.

4. If your prospects don't need or want what you are selling, refer them to a better resource.

5. You never know when a good deed may be returned. Relationship selling is referral business. There is no better way to get quality referrals than with help and honesty.

6. Manage relationships with follow up and service. Be sure clients get attention with follow up calls and deliver what you promise.

Relationship Sales Model

The relationships selling process has four levels or phases in order of importance:

1. Meeting and building a rapport and establishing trust

2. Asking questions and identify needs

3. Make a presentation

4. Closing the sale

Listen more than you talk, ask questions. Establish what you are selling is a benefit and a product or service fit. Work on building trust with honesty. Gain confidence that what you say is true.

The result is that what you sell will benefit the client. The last thing is to close the sale. If 1, 2 and 3 are successful closing the sale will be a natural continuation of the sales process.

The Hard Sell Sales Model

The hard sell model is the opposite of relationship selling. The least important concern is a relationship; the most important is getting to the close quickly. The hard sell sales model:

1. Does not build rapport, you tell the client what *you* think they need to know in order to sell them.

2. Your questions are not really questions but are sales qualifiers to determine what closing strategies will work best. You filter out what wastes time. You have little interest in clients needs as long as they buy.

3. You gloss over features and benefits only to hit sales points that you think will close the sale.

4. You try to close the sale like an 800-pound gorilla.

The difference between the strategies is the 'close at all costs' model is simply focused on spending time with customers to set up a close. The relationship model is setting up customer satisfaction and building relationships, the close becomes part of the process.

Building long-term relationships is smart business; it's a long-term success strategy. It keeps the door open for future business. Treat customers as you would have them treat you or you will not get a second opportunity to sell them anything.

Steps To Build Or Break Relationships

1. You are an ally to your customer and a trusted resource. However, if you put your needs, commission or sales quotas ahead of your customer, you may end the relationship.

2. Think us and we, not them.

3. Be proactive, make regular calls to customers and clients; do not wait for customers to call you.

4. Surprise your customers and deliver more than you promised instead of over promising and under delivering.

5. Be a problem solver and solution provider.

6. Mistakes happen. Take responsibility and work at fixing things quickly.

7. Treat customers as if they are life-long business partners.

Customer satisfaction keeps them coming back:

Keeping Customers Happy Is Both Offensive and Defensive Strategy

A satisfied customer keeps the competition out and drives repeat business. Load the sales odds in your favor. It's not rocket science, it's sixth grade math and common sense:

How to Grow Sales 101:

1. Lose Less

2. Sell More

A satisfied customer is virtually a guarantee of more success if you take advantage of the relationship. Satisfied customers give you a priceless edge. Recommendations and introductions from satisfied customers are valuable leads and new business opportunities.

Referrals And Introductions Are Insulin Pumps For Sellers

Be an expert at understanding your product. Know the marketplace and your competition. Understand your client needs. You are never out of the classroom. Relationship selling is non-stop learning for the seller. You must commit to being a new information machine to your clients and customers to maintain your relationship value.

Relationship selling also means you are virtually on your own. You must be self-motivated and directed. A company can help you by giving you tools but maintaining and building relationships is your job alone. Your success handling and dealing with clients is up to you:

Relationship Selling Is Managing Behavior As If You Own The Business

You must be pro-active on important details to stay on track. You must develop a system that works for you and not give your competitors an edge or reason to get in the door.

Relationship selling made me a top performer once I figured out what to do, how to do it and why customer satisfaction was so important. It led me to learning critical skills I used in running companies. Mastering relationships skills will make you a professional at every level of business.

You can do no better than become a master of service and develop an attitude of support. The paradox in sales is the more you give, the more earn.

You Earn a Living Selling, But You Can Make a Fortune Over a Lifetime Building Relationships and Friendships

How You
Think Is Everything

- Hard Closing Is An Outdated Industrial Age Sales Strategy

- Educated And Enlightened Customers May Know As Much As You About Your Product

- It's Not What You Know, It's Who You Know

- Make Yourself Likable, You'll Sell More

- Relationship Selling Is Customer Based And Problem Solving

CHAPTER 4

We're Wired For Stories: Telling And Selling

If you want to sell more, tell more tales. A good sales story stimulates the mind and engages people to conversation. If you are selling and people are not tuned to what you are saying, it's almost impossible to move them to action. Executives and world-class sellers tell stories to get people involved.

Stories are not more important than features and benefits; they help emphasize points and create feelings. Combining data and left-brain logic with emotional right-brain stories is a powerful and professional way to make dramatic sales points. Executives, politicians and professionals tell stories to start people thinking and make important points.

What sells people is how they see benefits working for them. Storytelling engages people in their *own minds, emotions and imagery*. Although decisions are largely *formed* with logic, data and information, decisions are mostly *made* with right-brain subjective emotions.

Storytelling is a strategic sophisticated sales tool. We know that people are going to forget data and information but are unlikely to forget a good story.

A good story defines relationships, a sequence of events, cause and effect, and a priority among items-and those elements are likely to be remembered as a complex whole.

—Gordon Shaw
Harvard Business Review

President Ronald Reagan exploited his age and was nearly 70 when he became president. He left office at 78, the oldest man ever to serve in the office. He joked about himself and repositioned a problem to an advantage with wit and humor:

One of my favorite quotations about age comes from Thomas Jefferson. He said that we should never judge a president by his age, only by his work. And ever since he told me that, I've stopped worrying, and just to show you how youthful I am, I intend to campaign in all 13 states.

Robert Kiyosaki, author of the Rich Dad, Poor Dad series has sold over 26,000,000 books since 1997 and has earned tens of millions of dollars. You may have read his books or seen him on TV. Three of his books, Rich Dad Poor Dad, Rich Dad's CASHFLOW Quadrant and Rich Dad's Guide to Investing, have been on the top 10 best-seller lists simultaneously in The Wall Street Journal, USA Today and the New York Times.

I have been friends with Robert over 28 years. He was my business associate in Honolulu and I was his business associate in La Jolla, California.

He produced a line of clothing for a radio station I managed and I produced seminars and workshops for him.

Much of the success of Rich Dad is not simply because Robert wrote a book. The message of becoming a better money manager, understanding taxes, dealing with expenses and using the power of leverage to create wealth *created a story that challenged conventional thought:* only high income leads to wealth.

Robert crafted a story of logic and emotion so he could repeat it virtually word for word in seminars and in radio, TV and newspaper interviews. He took a simple boring subject about money and made it visually and emotionally unique by telling a story.

The story of two fathers is an unusual message. Without that story, Rich Dad would have been like so many other books telling of money and investing. Robert is a gifted storyteller and his messages are motivating, entertaining and lead to his record-breaking success as an author.

- Are you successful because you simply sell a product?

- Do you master sales because people relate to you, your values and your knowledge?

- Do you get people emotionally involved?

- What makes you unique and a standout in a crowded field?

What Are Stories?

Stories are images and eye candy for the brain. Words are ways of communicating the images in the mind. When we tell stories well we are actually imagining what happens in the story and using words to describe what we see.

Remembering And Telling

Storytelling has a common problem. More salespeople would use stories if they could just remember how to tell the story.

It's the same problem in public speaking. Remembering words can stump people. People try to memorize things that are far too difficult to remember. Unless you have a photographic memory, remembering word for word is out of the question. That is why we invented computers, to keep track of lists and words.

To tell stories naturally, imagine what happens in the story. You can use the same words every time if that comes easily to you or you can use different words every time to tell a story. As long as you connect the words to the images in your mind, you can deliver a good story.

Three Keys To Storytelling

1. **Learn The Story.** Focus on the story and get the image in your mind. It is far easier to remember scenes or sequences of several images of things like sounds and pictures than the literal sequence of many hundreds of words. Remember, *it's never the story, it's always the emotion* that communicates the real meaning. Tell the story from your memory of how it made you feel.

2. **Telling The Story.** Relax, have fun and enjoy the story; it will be easier to tell. Imagine what is happening in the story. Use your natural style and expression.

3. **Remembering The Story.** You will not easily forget a good story. Images stay with you. However, words escape you. As long are you are confident that you do not have to remember word for word, the story will be easy to remember.

The Secrets Of Story Strategy

We tell stories in sales situations because it helps compel people to action. It is hard to make a computer chip exciting, a stack of lumber enthralling. That's why selling features and benefits are rarely enough to bring people to action. People make decisions in their minds, *not from your mind.* Draw pictures for people and reach them emotionally.

Use Stories As Sales Tools:

1. Use stories to keep ideas in order and show ideas sequentially: First this happened and then that happened

2. Use stories to point out how this happened or that happened

3. Use stories to help others understand why things happen

4. Use stories to share information and to illustrate

5. Use stories to help illustrate principles that can be used in other situations

Stories Stimulate Even More Stories

Have you noticed people clamoring to tell you their story before you finish your story? When people listen to your story, *they are actually visualizing their story.*

Stories stimulate more stories and start conversation. You learn a lot from talking to people and when people tell you their stories, you learn even more about them.

If people don't talk back to you, you will have a problem selling them anything. Passive listeners may be thinking about dinner or picking up the dog from the veterinarian. Even worse, they may be thinking, "when is this presentation ever going to end?"

A client telling you a story is very likely the one to be telling you to write down orders. A storytelling client is an order waiting to happen! Remember that features and benefits are boring but people engaged in a story are emotionally connecting to you.

People see things through their paradigms. Be sure your story develops not simply from your point of view but a story that will stimulate a positive associate idea in others.

What sells people on your story is not your story, it's how they interpret the story for their own benefit or viewpoint. A story should not simply jump out of your mouth. *It should be constructed to achieve your objective.*

The key to crafting a story is the logical flow. It must have a beginning, middle and end. However, it needs a trigger to set off an emotion. The trigger can be something that will literally force the prospect to ask a question. A trigger can set off ideas of what to buy, when to buy and how to buy because your story is compelling.

How To Craft A Story

- Start with simple recognizable truths
- Show the way out of problems and situations
- Show how customers win

- Show why your products or service works better than competitors

- Show why your products or service has more value

- Use scenarios of what and why to make things work and happen

- Leave room for the listener to have their own points of view

- Have fun telling stories, be real, be alive

What will make you a great storyteller will be how well you craft stories to fit situations.

Ad-libbing stories without following an outline and strategic thinking may be hit-and-miss. Without a roadmap in your mind, *a story told differently every time might have a different meaning every time.*

You may be adding things that will get you off track, forgetting important ideas and getting yourself into twists that may alter the outcome. Critically, you may miss using an emotional trigger in the right place. You cannot expect the best results if you wing stories.

Develop a bank of stories that you can use to illustrate important points, scenarios, answer objections and show benefits though real-life situations or people and how others can meet their needs from your stories.

The following is a story that I used to tell. It helped me to sell tens of thousands of dollars of radio advertising to small advertisers who never thought they could afford to advertise. I was selling for WLYF FM Radio in Miami and a small account called to ask about advertising on the radio.

Rid O' Rust

The Story Of A Radio Commercial That Magically Appeared On Television

A company called Rid O' Rust called the WLYF radio office. They asked to have a salesperson come to their office and explain how radio advertising worked and how much it would cost. Given the sales lead, I went to meet the owner of the company.

As soon as I arrived at their office, the prospect told me about his service and the problem of getting new business.

"I need to find a way to market my product better," he told me and began to tell me a story.

In South Florida, homes use sprinkler water systems to keep lawns green. As the water table is shallow and near the surface of the ground, putting in a well is simple. You drill down to the underground water level and put the pipe in the ground. For years, the common pipes used in wells were made of iron. However, in time the iron pipes leached rust.

When sprinkler systems turned on, water sitting in the well pipe pumped through the system. If a lawn came up to the edge of the house, sprinklers watering the grass sprayed water on the side of house as well.

The rusty well water was hardly noticeable at first but reddish brown stains began to appear on the side of houses.

Rid O' Rust had a device that allowed a small amount of rust-neutralizing chemical to mix with the water as it came out of the sprinklers. When the sprinklers turned on, the chemical automatically added to the water and stains slowly went away. The Rid O' Rust service came to the house and refilled the bottles of stain neutralizer.

"All the advertising I tried so far has not really worked. Could radio help?" the owner asked.

I said I thought it may work but it was going to take a creative radio commercial to explain the service. Together we calculated the tiny advertising budget and figured he could afford only six radio commercials a week for four weeks. If the advertising produced results, he could continue the schedule.

I went back to the radio station and told our creative people the kind of commercial we needed. A 60-second radio spot commercial was created.

"Does your house have those ugly brown stains from your sprinkler system? Does it look like your house has been painted with brown paint? Would you like to see those stains go away in just a few weeks?"

The soft background music in the commercial helped the radio announcer sound sincere. When you heard that commercial, you could actually visualize brown stains on houses. The message was simple but very effective.

I Didn't Know Radio Had Pictures

The client approved the radio commercials and they began to run over the air. I was on appointments and got back to the radio station late in the afternoon. Our account assistant told me we had a good response to the new Rid O' Rust advertiser.

People were calling to get the phone number of the company so they could order the service. However, the strange thing was people were saying they had just seen the commercial on TV.

Some listeners said they saw it on WLYF TV. I said how interesting, we have no WLYF television station in Miami.

I went to the production studio and asked to hear the Rid O' Rust commercial that played on the air earlier in the day. I listened to the commercial and there was no mention of a TV station in the advertising script.

The next day I waited in the office for the commercial to run on the air. I wanted to see if we would get more calls and I wanted to hear what people were saying first hand. The commercial ran and within minutes, we had people calling about Rid O' Rust.

People were asking, "What's the phone number of Rid O' Rust, we just saw that commercial and we don't remember the phone number."

"I just saw it on WLYF TV," some people said.

Hearing this for myself, I was confused. I called Rid O' Rust and asked, "Are you running advertising on a television station in Miami?" The answer was no other advertising was being done except on the radio station.

As the week went on, the radio station continued to get similar phone calls every time the commercial ran. I called the account. He told me they were getting lots of new customers and most of them mentioned *seeing the commercial* while a few said they heard it on WLYF radio.

Seeing With Ears

People responding to the advertising did not see a Rid O' Rust commercial on TV. The radio commercial created a reality in their minds. People were seeing what they wanted to see and hearing what they wanted to hear.

I realized what was causing the confusion.

At the time Rid O' Rust commercials were running on the radio station, WLYF Radio was running television ads promoting people to tune to WLYF Radio.

The soundtracks of the TV ads were virtually the same sound tracks the announcers used on the radio station. Both the radio station and the TV commercials were saying the same thing over and over, "WLYF IS BEAUTIFUL, W-L-Y-F FM. ALL MUSIC, ALL THE TIME."

People seeing WLYF Radio ads on TV were also listeners to the radio station. They were hearing the same message on both the radio and on TV.

When the descriptive Rid O' Rust advertising ran on the radio station, people put TV and Radio together in their minds. What they heard became a picture. People were confused yet convinced Rid O' Rust was a television advertiser.

I Told the Story Over and Over

The Rid O' Rust story was my best small account sales closer. The fun simple story was true, believable and it opened up real discussions.

People drew their own conclusions why the advertising and marketing worked. They felt confident if a company like Rid O' Rust could get results, they could as well.

I took advertising orders on the spot. Many times people were so excited they wanted to write their own radio advertising copy.

The key to storytelling is in the invitation for listeners to become involved with you. Real authentic conversations are an exchange of ideas and a giant step forward in closing sales.

Get Everyone In On Those Great Sales Stories

Companies help salespeople learn a pitch or presentation, yet few companies provide sales stories. If you are new to a company, go to people who have a proven record of accomplishment. Ask them about their experiences if they will share success stories.

If you're a sales veteran and need new ideas, a sales team can brainstorm and come up with new experiences that can be shared.

Send notes around the company and get executives involved, they will have new and different stories sellers can retell. People in your company don't have to be in sales to have a good story.

One of the best ways to improve storytelling style and improve techniques is to hear others tell stories. It's one thing to read a story but it is something else to hear a good story presented.

Sellers on the go and in the car have time to hear stories. MP3 players, iPods or any way of recording sales stories electronically and conveniently works. Transfer sale stores to audio files for podcasts and put them on the internet or send email files to salespeople.

Share more than one story. Compile as many successful sales stories as possible and make them available to everyone. Get twenty or thirty good stories on audio file and keep the stories current and fresh.

What helps salespeople become great storytellers is repetition. Presenting is a learned skill. If you hear a story over and over, in time, you pick up style, tempo and learn from example. Nothing will help you learn to story tell better than hearing others tell stories over and over until you can finally make their story your story.

Make storytelling a part of everyday selling. It brings boring data, charts and information to life and adds action, emotion and images. Storytelling adds a professional touch to any presentation.

People Buy Into Stories:

Master The Art Of Telling And Selling

How You Think Is Everything

- **Storytelling Stimulates Emotions**
- **It's Easy To Remember And Tell Stories If You Don't Focus On The Words**
- **Storytelling Is Strategic Selling**
- **Stories Enable Clients To Relate To You And Your Story Through Their Eyes**
- **Stories Evoke More Stories And Soon Enough, Clients Are Telling You Stories**
- **Stories Make People Human And Natural**
- **Share Your Stories With Audio Files**

CHAPTER 5

Negotiating
And Renegotiating

Who is a negotiator?

Look In The Mirror

Supply and demand drives markets. The balance of power shifts from one side to another. If supply is high, buyers have the upper hand and prices fall. If supply is low, customers bid up prices and sellers are in control.

When products are hot, sellers have an easy time making sales and reaching quota. High demand makes selling easy. However, when buyers are in control, it may be time to launch a different sales strategy where the best outcome may be through negotiating.

How It Works

Selling is performing the art of persuading.

Negotiating is interaction to resolve differences.

When prospects say NO, you continue to sell, walk away or you may find yourself in a position to start negotiating your sale.

Negotiating works towards agreement and the rules are different from selling. Sellers may find themselves negotiating because it may be the only way to get the business. In times of high supply, buyers and consumers take advantage of opportunity, the new slogan becomes what experienced investors, traders, business people and lawyers know:

You Can Negotiate Anything

The buyer's job is to get the best value and prices they can at the time. Buyers are trained to negotiate; this is their opportunity. Consumers may not have professional negotiation training but this doesn't stop them from trying to get better deals, they just take a different path.

Consumers are increasingly cost conscious because of competition and inflation. If consumers do not like retail store pricing the next stop is Costco, Wal-Mart, a discounter or the internet for more variety and better prices.

Many will forgo the frills, nice displays, fancy fixtures or a piano playing at the end of the staircase to save money. This has everything to do with the sales climate of today. A bigger economy with more people creates more buying as well as selling opportunities.

While many companies make all-time record profits, others are profit squeezed and cash short. They try to find ways to cut expenses to the bone and focus on price points.

The pressure is on sellers to sell more as companies pay attention to consumers needs. Products and services sold efficiently means more sellers will be negotiating sales.

Negotiating Secrets

The paradox of speed in negotiating may lead to unprofitable deals. Things happen fast in business but that has little to do with negotiating sales. Negotiating is a game of strategic skills; *it's a process.*

A Tale Of Two Frogs

Two frogs fell into a deep cream bowl,
One was an optimistic soul,
But the other took a gloomy view,
We shall drown he cried, without more adieu!

So with a last despairing cry,
He flung up his legs and said "goodbye"

Said the frog with a merry grin,
I can't get out, but I won't give in,
I'll just swim around till my strength is spent,
Then I will die the more content.

Bravely he swam till it did seem,
His struggling began to churn the cream,

On top of the butter at last he stepped,
And out of the bowl at last he leapt.

What of the moral? 'Tis easily found,
If you can't get out... keep swimming around!

Negotiating Goals

Priorities must be set in advance. In negotiating, you must be able to focus, concentrate and follow the "negotiating game." Never get into a sales negotiation without knowing what you want to accomplish. Know what you want before you start.

More often than not, the negotiating winner will be the one with the best skills, *not the person with the best position.*

Negotiating "Rules of the game" are non-existent so don't bother looking for them. Rules are made up as you go along. If you cannot think on the fly, you may find yourself over your head. That is why your selling parameters are set before you start negotiations. The key in sales negotiating:

The Will To Win Is To Prepare

Negotiation is like football. The goal line is where you want to get but you are going to have a hard time making a beeline for it. It might take yard after yard of grinding effort to make progress or it can happen on one big play.

Negotiating success will depend on how prepared you are and how you think on your feet. These are very different rules than selling and persuading others to buy things.

Negotiating Is Not Fair or Democratic:

You Get What You Negotiate, Not What You Deserve

Buyers Go On Offense

A classic position of buyers is a tactic to put sellers on notice, "I don't have to buy from you." It may be intimidating to face this attitude but do not let it put you on defensive; **it is a ploy and a tactic to get you off guard.**

If a buyer or prospect is at the negotiating table, they are there for one reason. They believe they have something to gain. Arrogance and aggressive behavior on either side is a weak position but people often try to bully their way to get what they want.

Do not be quick to show your insight, knowledge and preparation. Do not put everything on the table right away. Timing is important in negotiation; take the time to understand others and their positions. Tipping your hat to your negotiating ability may get others working harder to beat you. Take your time until you have gathered all the information.

You Cannot Argue with a Stone Wall

When people take a position in negotiation and refuse to waver, you may have hit a dead end. When you discover where others' interests lie, you may have found a place to start compromising and resolving issues.

Getting people off a position is difficult unless you understand why they have taken that position. In sales negotiations, some will take things for granted and do not ask an important question:

Why?

When you discover why people ask for what they want, you may be a lot closer to finding a resolution and making a sale.

A firm position or demand is a stone wall you cannot argue with. Find out what is *behind* the wall. Listen intently until you discover why the other party is at the table so you can negotiate issues that matter and not waste time.

Insight will make the difference and people skills will most likely be your strongest asset in negotiating. Everyone has different personality styles and traits. Determine how *your* behavior impacts others and adjust your style and behavior accordingly. Communication success is how well you relate and interface with others.

You're Not A Psychoanalyst

It's simple to understand others' behavior and personality styles as long as you don't try to over think and play psychoanalyst. People are far too complex to figure out so don't waste your time trying. You do not want to set off personality alarms when you negotiate; it will take you off your purpose to make a sale.

The idea is to get along with others so you can keep focused on negotiating and not personal issues. You will find that virtually in every case, people will have a dominate trait fitting one of following four styles:

Common Behavior Personality Styles:

The Controlling Style, aggressive, dominant, get it done now, "it's my way or the highway"

The Reserved Style, steady, methodical, team player

The Talkative Style, influencing, tries to motivate others, wants you to like them

The Introverted Style, cautious, conscientious, detail oriented, "show me how" attitude

People may change their dominant style or use a combination of styles to accommodate a situation. Be patient. In time, people's personalities show through, especially under stress.

Have this thought in mind when you get into negotiations, it is a people skills game: what kind of communicators are they and what kind of personality styles do they have? Look for the style and adjust to it but do not over think it and do not make it obvious.

You cannot change what you are and people may see through you if you try. However, you can subtly *adjust* your style and that may be all it takes to make you a much better negotiator. The end game is to keep personality friction from blocking the negotiating and sales process.

How To Adjust To Different Styles:

Aggressive Personalities. They want fast answers and no flowers. Get to the value and sales points quickly, no chitchats.

Talkative and People Oriented. Be friendly and social but do not underestimate them. They may be trying to sell you to their positions and talk you out of yours.

Good Listeners. Be calm and steady as they are reserved. Slow down and control enthusiasm. Still water may run deep. Be cautious of thoughtful listeners.

Introverted and Sticklers for Detail. Be factual and specific. Everything you say may be challenged. Don't overreact. Choose words and details carefully.

Tone of voice and body language are keys to understanding people. Be alert, listen intently and watch closely. Keep your eyes on who you are negotiating with. Pick up clues to how they feel about what they are saying.

The #1 Negotiating Skill Is Active Listening

This is how professional sale negotiators win; it has very little to with negotiation positions and everything to do with negotiating skills.

Let others talk more; they may talk themselves into a corner.

Never Interrupt Others
When They Are Making Mistakes

When you listen more, you are able to collect your thoughts and be less likely to make mistakes.

Your communication skills and ability to read others will be your strongest assets in sales negotiating.

The 12 Steps To Better Negotiating:

1. **Listen Intently.** *Active listening* is the #1 skill in sales negotiating. LISTEN! Realize that most people are trained to talk at people. Use that knowledge to your advantage. You need to listen.

2. **Prepare To Win Or Be Sure To Lose.** Prepare, prepare, prepare.

3. **Know What You Want, Aim High.** Do not be afraid to ask for more. Be an optimist and it will be a self-fulfilling prophecy.

4. **Find Out What The Other Side Wants.** The other side would not be there if they had nothing to gain. What are they after and how can you help them meet their needs? *Ask open-ended questions.*

5. **Do Not Make Unilateral Concessions.** Never open sales negotiations with discounts. Don't offer across the board deals like a flat 10% discount unless you get agreements to buy more or they buy different products or services in addition to earn the discount. ***"Lets work together,"*** is far different from, ***"Anything you want."***

6. **There Is Power In Your Walk-Away Alternative.** You never disclose this and never threaten. At what point will you walk away is your secret. If you put that on the negotiating table, it may be perceived as arrogance.

7. **Do Not Allow Others To Intimidate You.** Your point of view or issues are not less important because you are selling and they are buying.

8. **Be Patient. Try Not To Make The First Move.** You may jump the gun before you understand the game. It is virtually impossible to negotiate if the pressure is on to get the order or do a deal immediately.

9. **Be Suspicious Of Deadlines.** They may be phony and a ploy to pressure you into making a bad decision if time runs out.

10. **Be Reasonable And Flexible.** Look for a satisfying agreement for both parties.

11. **Negotiation Is A Process Not An Event.** Remember the frog in the bowl of cream.

12. **Deal Honestly And Ethically.** Deal with integrity; you may need future opportunities to negotiate with the same buyers or customers.

Renegotiating

With fast moving technology in competitive business conditions, things change quickly.

Competition may re-position your product or service. Things may have to be renegotiated even when both sides do not want to.

It would be nice to think you can sell things and that is the end of the story. However, if you sales are open-ended, anything can happen.

Companies spend big money undoing what has been done. In today's litigious world, the only thing you can count on is money in the bank *after the check clears.*

Can't Do What We Promised!

What makes renegotiations different from negotiations is you have experience with people. Your job is to figure out why a commitment has changed. One of the oldest lines you may hear is, "It's not personal, it's just business."

When I hear that bomb coming, it's just another way of saying, "We need the money more than you," or "We paid you too much and your competitor is offering a better deal."

In almost every case, "It's only business," is simply bad behavior and a sign of fast changing times and intense competition.

Renegotiations *Are* Personal

Every thing in business is personal if it has to do with your salary, commissions or bonus. Since when is losing money impersonal? If you suffer personal damage for someone's lack of integrity and commitment, it certainly is personal.

However, people and companies do get in trouble; your customer may need help. You have to determine what a real problem is and what is not. When things change, it's a problem for both *you and the client.*

You get out your renegotiation suit because as soon as the lawyers get involved, the money meter starts running, commissions are lost and in almost ever case, the only winners are the lawyers.

I have never personally seen a company want to get in a lawsuit for fun. If you go to the legal ring and start to battle, chances of future business and relationships are over. However, that may be unavoidable.

The win/win theory of business is more a good idea than a reality. Most often than not, it is one or the other side saying, "I won more and you didn't do so well."

Companies are dependent on long-term relationships and repeat business. However, commission structures, incentives and bonuses may incentivize salespeople to short-term goals. In some situations, customers might not benefit from short-term selling practices and this may create longer-term problems.

Renegotiating is more often than not damage control. Think strategically and not emotionally; look for plausible solutions:

- Can you reduce the current agreement to save the order and get more in the future?

- Can you lower the price and get more business to make up for the loss?

- Can you sell an additional product to take the place of the renegotiated price?

You can't forecast a train wreck but you can buy insurance and hedge your bet with diversification and more sales. Salespeople are more and more likely to find themselves in negotiating and renegotiating situations. Mastering negotiating skills is a career skill that will help you make profitable sales today and it's the must-have skill of the future.

Alert sales and marketing people see new forces at work in business, marketing and sales. As companies look for ever-increasing profits in more competitive times, top performing sellers become even more valuable, especially sellers with strong negotiation skills.

How You
Think Is Everything

- Negotiation Is A Learned Skill

- Selling Generates Revenue But Negotiating May Determine Profits

- Negotiations Are Not About How To Sell Things Cheaper

- Negotiating Has A Speed Limit, Most Often You Can't Do It Fast *And* Do It Well

- Negotiations More Often Are Won With Communication Skills

- Negotiating Is Listening Actively, Not Fast Talking

- Renegotiating Is A Fact Of Life In Competitive Fast Changing Times

CHAPTER 6

Everyone Is Already Motivated

Motivation can be tricky. What motivates each of us changes daily throughout our lives. The key to understanding motivation is that everyone is uniquely different. When it comes to motivation, it's not a good idea to assume anything.

People buy for different reasons than what you may be thinking. People are complex and complicated. However, four basic factors motivate the vast majority:

1. **Profit**. Money, wealth and income.

2. **Internal.** Moral, philanthropy, civic duty and intellect.

3. **Recognition.** Respect, admiration and acknowledgement.

4. **Power.** Control, independence, competition and victory.

The secret to selling others is insight. Insight comes from understanding that motivation is like a one-way mirror. You see out but others cannot see in. Not understanding principles on how motivation works may lead you to see only a reflection of your own thoughts:

Myth #1: You can motivate me.

Myth #2: I can motivate you.

Ever since I began selling, I was told the big success would come from my ability to motivate others. Yet all the time I was thinking, something is wrong with this picture. I knew I was motivated to do things for my reasons. I did things for others to get to my goals. However, when others told me they were going to motivate me, I became defensive. I instinctively understood the myth of motivation.

I was successful in selling and managing for almost 20 years before I figured out I was right. I should have trusted my instincts.

A series of business workshops led me to professional training and understanding people, personalities and motivation. I realized that much of my success was simply bubbly personality, drive, energy and massive persistence. I was stumbling on to sales as much as professionally earning them.

I could have been more effective had I understood the principles of motivation and not relied on being a light bulb with a lampshade on my head.

I had more brawn and energy than knowledge. However, once I learned the insider's secrets of motivation, I was able to improve my managing and sales performance. I began to look at what made people do what they did.

You cannot change what motivates others. You can only manipulate them with money, prizes, incentives, recognition, power or any number of things. You can get others to do what you want but that has nothing to do with their personal motivation.

The fastest and best way to get others to do what you want is create an atmosphere or change the environment to allow others to motivate themselves. It's that simple, although it may not be that easy.

People Buy Things Because Of Their Wants, Needs and Reasons, Not Yours

Only customer's goals count. When you create an environment that allows others to get what they want, your sales improve.

As a professional seller, you must deal with your ego that often says you move others to take action. The reality is *you cannot motivate others* but the good news is right in front of your face. Simply transfer your energies and take advantage of an important fact:

Everybody Is Already Motivated

If you determine what motivates others, you sell more effectively. The basic tenet to motivation is inside of us. Internal motivation is longer lasting and more self-directed. External motivation is reinforced with rewards, praise, recognition and incentives.

If the cat is away, the mice will play. The cat remembers you because you bring catnip and treats on a regular basis; cats, like customers, are fickle. Clients left to their own devices may change their minds.

If you don't understand wants and needs, you may not understand why people do things. Sales relationships and alignments grow stronger over time when the right sales buttons are pushed.

Motivation principles are hardly a secret, yet few use this powerful sales tool to advantage. Presidents, CEOs, politicians and top executives use the principles repeatedly. Motivation principles have everything to do with **active listening skills.**

Write down the following principles. These rules are powerful sales guides of excellent sellers; they adhere to the most basics and critical of all sales principles. Focus on what will motivate others to take action:

Keep a copy of these principles with you.

Motivational Principles:

1. You *cannot motivate* other people.

2. *All people* are motivated.

3. People do things for *their reasons*, not your reasons.

4. A person's *strength overused* may become their weakness.

5. The very best one can do to motivate others is to *create an environment* that allows specific individuals to motivate themselves.

1. **You Cannot Motivate Other People:** You have no control over others. However, you can get people to do things for your reasons because they either:

A. Have to

B. Want to

People need to achieve and make decisions from desires within.

2. **All People Are Motivated.** All people do things because of personal reasons. Some people are highly energized and all they need is motive and opportunity. They are motivated and off to the races. Others may be slow to react but once they get moving, they may run and be energetic. People move towards their goals, not yours.

3. **People Do Things For Their Reasons, Not Your Reasons.** WIIFM is not a radio or TV station, it's "What's In It For Me." We sell others by showing them *what is in it for them.* We appeal to logic, emotion, rewards, recognition, pride, achievement and common sense. People don't buy because we want them to buy. *They buy for their reasons.* The sales job is to figure out what motivates others to make buying decisions.

4. **A Person's Strength Overused May Become Their Weakness.** The hardest person to understand is ourselves. We use our strengths because we become comfortable with

our success. However, our strength overused may become a weakness or Achilles heel. Being a gifted speaker is strength, but talking too much is a weakness. A high IQ is an asset but an uncontrollable smart mouth is a weakness.

5. **The Best One Can Do To Motivate Others Is Create An Environment That Allows Specific Individuals To Motivate Themselves.** You can only create an environment that encourages and promotes self-motivation. The sales challenge is to give people a reason to *want to buy and satisfy a need they have.* That is why the greatest strength of a seller is the ability to listen and understand others. Environment means both mental and physical. You may be able to change a no sale to a customer by simply helping others build self-esteem. Everyone is uniquely individual. Ask questions, listen and learn. Discover what motivates your prospects and customers.

Change Your Attitude To Gain Altitude

First, look to yourself and change your attitude towards others. People like to be heard, recognized and acknowledged:

Accepting The Individuality Of Others Is A Sign Of Your Strength, Not Weakness

You are a more effective salesperson respecting the rights and thoughts of others.

You may be trying to motivate others with your strategies, tactics and ideas but in the end, they will buy for their reasons.

Professional sellers have figured out what cowboys said in movies years ago is true, "You can lead a horse to water but you cannot make it drink." Learn to position the principles of motivation as a strategic tool to maximize your sales potential.

How You
Think Is Everything

- It's A Myth That You Can Motivate Others

- People Are Motivated Internally

- People Do Things For Their Reasons, Not Your Reasons

- Change The Environment And You Can Change Motivation

- Focus On Helping Others Get What They Want For Their Reasons

- Keep Your Sales Ego In Control

CHAPTER 7

How Fast Can You Learn?

Company Perspective:

Salespeople must be educated in the value of the product or service. In a competitive marketplace, sales training gives the seller effective tools to use and companies get a return on investment.

Salespersons Perspective:

Salespeople know the importance of mastering product and market knowledge. They will make reasonable efforts to learn as much as they need. Salespeople see the company's obligation is to provide training and all the support they need.

Top Performing Salespersons Perspective:

Top Performers do not stop learning at product training. Their sales job is 24/7, not nine to five. They recognize personal skills as the critical difference to top performance. They own these skills. They have no problem investing time and money for their own education to improve themselves to achieve top performance selling.

The Difference

A company provides seller's a product or service. However, top performers do not think of themselves as sales commodities or simply, sellers. They see themselves as executives responsible for the revenue department. They know companies will pay top dollar for top performance so they go all out to reach the top ranks.

The average seller will do what is necessary to perform the job but that's were it stops. They are not willing to take the time and money to develop themselves.

Sellers Do A Job
Top Performers Master Skills

Common Commodities

In a competitive market, common job skills may become a common commodity. That lowers the value and income for salespeople. Unless salespeople are able to add unique personal values, they will have little competitive edge.

Investor's Business Daily (IBD) is a leading newspaper for investors and business leaders. I have been reading it for years and find well-informed investing advice and articles on leadership, management, marketing, research and sales published in their pages.

The newspaper goes beyond money and investing. It analyzes successful people across all lifestyles and occupations. *IBD* follows what makes leaders, investors, businesspeople, entrepreneurs and salespeople winners.

IBD rules will help average salespeople become better business people and stronger sellers:

IBD's 10 Secrets To Success

1. **How You Think Is Everything.** Be positive. Think success, not failure. Avoid negative people and environments.

2. **Decide On Your Dreams And Goals.** Be specific about your goals and write them down, develop a plan to reach them.

3. **Take Action.** Goals are nothing without action. Don't be afraid to get started. Just do it.

4. **Never Stop Learning.** Go back to school, read books, acquire new skills.

5. **Be Persistent And Work Hard.** Success is a marathon, not a sprint. Never give up.

6. **Learn To Analyze Details.** Get all the facts, all the input. Learn from your mistakes.

7. **Focus Your Time And Money.** Don't let people or things distract you.

8. **Don't Be Afraid To Innovate; Be Different.** Following the crowd is a path to mediocrity.

9. **Deal And Communicate With People Effectively.** No person is an island. Learn to understand and motivate others.

10. **Be Honest And Dependable; Take Responsibility.** Otherwise, numbers 1-9 won't matter.

Your Sales Future Is Now

Beginning sales jobs pay beginner's wages. As sales jobs become more demanding, responsibility increases and the stakes go higher. Higher sales income eventually follows.

A trained nurse makes a good income. A nurse's job is important and the service to the community is valuable. However, nurses do not have the same responsibility as a doctor who has spent years in college and medical school, practiced and interned before they became professional.

Both the nurse and the doctor are in the medical profession. One makes a good income, but the other makes 15 to 30 times more. Both serve an important need, however, doctors are trusted to diagnose and treat.

Top performing salespeople perform much like a doctor and not only sell; they may be the ones to save company lives.

Today's competitive business conditions are the best times for top end salespeople. **As competition increases, the need for increased revenues and top performing salespeople follows.**

It's A Process

Developing skills takes time. You focus on learning what the top 20 percent of salespeople do. Follow the winners' lead as they have learned how to sell 80 percent of the revenue. If you follow what average sellers do, you will have average income and career results.

The Pareto 80-20 Principle

The 80-20 rule known to most in sales is the law of the vital few. It points out that 20 percent of the sellers will make 80 percent of the sales.

Joseph M. Juran thought of the principle and named it after Italian economist Vilfredo Pareto who saw that 80 percent of income in Italy went to 20 percent of the population.

In 2005, the top 1 percent of tax returns in the U.S. paid 39.4 percent of all federal individual income taxes. One percent of wealthiest in the U.S. earned 21.2 percent of all income. That is the law of the vital few.

In every sales situation I worked, I have seen the 80-20 rule in action. It's predictable enough you can almost bet on it. The more salespeople performing the same job in the same circumstances, the more accurate the Pareto principle becomes.

You Get It Or You Don't

In sales, either you get the business or you don't. You win or lose. A sale earns company revenue. A lost sale does not earn income for you or the company.

Even though losing a sale may have been a close call, the #2 sale is still the 1st place loser. Winning by a little does not count as a partial win. You win if you win.

Selling is measured. The outcome is numbers and performance. Selling is not political or theory. To improve your career and income, don't bother asking for more money or a better job. Instead, learn how to sell more by improving your personal skills.

A company can only train you so much or give you so much support. If you want more income and a faster moving career, **Boost Your Sales!**

Tactical Vs. Strategic

Tactical salespeople go after the low hanging fruit and quick sales. They do not focus on meaningful relationships or learning more skills. They hit and run as fast as they can to make quick money and keep the job. Tactical salespeople are external and look for things to happen to them. After all, it's only a job.

Strategic salespeople take quick sales in stride but think long term. They work to gain knowledge and better quality clients that are more productive. Long-term thinking delivers trust and value to customers.

Sellers relying on personality and attitude win part of the time but get in trouble quickly when dealing with difficult complex issues.

Sales Charm Is Not Enough To Deal With Sophisticated Problems

The way to go from tactical short-term survival mode to strategic professional selling is master skills of professional sellers. Do what the pros do until you learn enough to do it better.

Few things will rev up sale skills faster than learning from a pro first hand. Remember the Pareto 80-20 rule and don't get your lessons from the average. Get your knowledge and ideas from the top performers.

I learned from the best because I asked for help from the best. I didn't wait for things to come to me and you should do the same.

If you're not in the top ranks, ask people who are willing to share how they do it. Learn strategies that work in real-life, not theory.

Drive Your Manager Nuts

I was a pain to sales managers I worked for. I constantly asked questions. When I was a top seller, I went to workshops and seminars to learn how to sell more. I was paying for my specialized sales knowledge. While the companies I worked for benefited from my education, the skills and knowledge I learned belonged to me.

Different people do it different and have different ideas. *You mold ideas and strategies to your style.* You cannot parrot or mimic scripts at higher levels of selling. Reciting canned pitches is for amateurs.

Use Your Unique Style And Personality

Time is the one thing sellers are always short of. That is because time may be managing us and we are not in control. To grow in sales is to make the commitment to take time away from a busy day to learn more to help long-term success.

Salespeople Read?

Salespeople will not read. While it's not true of all salespeople, it fits the majority. Forget about salespeople reading what is new and happening, they won't even read what is already published. It has nothing to do with IQ or intelligence; it's an occupational thing. Selling attracts busy people and they are more likely to be scan readers than document digesters. Their lives are on the run.

Many in sales are time-pressured, impatient and forced to read heavy detailed product documents that make reading a chore. For the most part, salespeople prefer fast reading short documents, short paragraphs, lots of bullet points and hyperlinks. It saves time.

However, not all books are long-winded and hard to comprehend and listening to audio while driving is a great way to learn new ideas and stay current.

Everything is moving so fast and changing, it's a challenge to keep up. If you make no effort and take your skills and knowledge for granted, it will not be long before you are behind the curve as new information and knowledge passes you by.

Diversity and other viewpoints will make you more knowledgeable. It will be hard to build relationships with clients and customers if your interests are simply in your product or service. Read and learn outside your field and read at least one book a quarter. That is hardly a challenge.

Get at least one subscription to a business magazine to keep up with what is going on in the economy and business world. Business articles on management, news and personal business will keep you up to date with your business savvy clients.

Having an edge is what it takes to become a professional. To improve in sales, you do not have to be miles ahead of others but you must be ahead of the pack and not stuck in the middle.

Read, learn and do not take your skills for granted or you will not maintain a competitive edge. Want to make more money in sales and boost your career?

Don't Stop Learning!

How You Think Is Everything

- Don't Stop Learning New Skills

- Begin Your Own Tradition-Read More

- Stay On The Leading Edge Or Risk Become A Common Commodity

- Define Your Difference Through Skills And Knowledge Or Others Will Define You As Average

- Personal Skills You Master Are Your Edge And Go Where You Go

- Learn More To Live Better

PART II

The Essential Sales Skills

Top performers make selling look easy. They seem to do things second nature. Second nature comes from practice. Practicing separates sales amateurs from professionals.

Tiger Woods is a natural athlete. He makes playing golf look like a walk in the park. However, Tiger was pounding golf balls hours on end since he was 18 months old before he became a "natural."

Frank Sinatra was one of the greatest singers of all time. His natural voice was pitch perfect and made singing look so easy anyone could do it, but no one could. Frank practiced voice control by holding his head under water as long as he could to control his breathing. He mastered the basics before he became known as "The Voice."

People are not born artists, presenters, programmers, leaders, entrepreneurs, CEOs or salespeople. You don't become a top performing salesperson simply because you have a winning personality. People get into sales and then get drummed out fast because they don't get what to do. It takes skills to win.

Selling needs practice and follow through. The more you sell, the more you practice, the better you get. Selling is a process and takes time to learn. When you master the basics, they will become habit and successful selling will become second nature.

CHAPTER 8

The Secret Is Not Presenting: It's Presenting Well

Skillful presenters go to the head of the class. The better presenter you are, the more you will find yourself presenting again. Presenting well means opportunity to make more sales.

Most salespeople have experience limited to one-on-one presenting. Many sellers avoid speaking in public. Public speaking and large-scale presentation turns stomachs and creates anxiety. Most salespeople are afraid to present or get up in front of a group even though they make a living selling ideas and influencing others.

The secret in public speaking and presenting is not as hard as it appears. With a few tips, you can dramatically improve your confidence. Prepare a road map to keep you on course and you can learn how to be a dynamic presenter. Once you catch on to presenting and speaking in public, you may go out of your way to do more.

The more you speak in public, the more **you** gain. The more people who know you by your presenting ability, the more it will lead to sales opportunities.

Contemporary Speaking

The Set Up

This tip will set you up to win because you will be in control. When speaking to a group or in public, never introduce yourself. Have others introduce you and sing your praises. Others saying things about you is ten times more powerful than anything you can say about yourself, company or product.

The way to avoid mistakes, embarrassment and a poor start is you write your own introduction. You put exactly what you want your audience to hear in writing. Prepare a short introduction on 5 ½ X 8 cardstock paper.

Remember that someone has to read what you write so write LARGE. Be sure others can read the script without holding it close to their face.

What you put on the card is:

1. What are your credentials (who are you)

2. Why are you making this presentation

3. What will people learn

Practice your scripted introduction in front of others and be sure it's dynamic but short and to the point.

Hand your introduction to the person who will introduce you giving them adequate time to read the script. Explain that you expect no changes and no adlibs and please read what is on the card with enthusiasm.

That is the only guaranteed way you get a good start to your presentation providing the reader will deliver your script professionally.

Spill The Beans

The first thing you do is smile, be friendly and establish immediately what you will be speaking about. Tell people what they will learn. This will give people anticipation how you will solve problems or create opportunities and how you will deliver the goods.

Get attention quickly to establish yourself so get right to the meat of the story. Create excitement or your audience will begin to wander.

If you present with a computer, turn off the screen **as soon as you make your points.** If you do not turn off the screen, people will not focus on you and they will miss what you say.

Computer presentations make it too easy to transfer data to slides and charts. Be careful not to overload people with endless charts and data, it will put them to sleep.

The idea is to make sales and money, not distribute information. If you cannot make the connection of what you present, you will miss your sales points. People forget 50 percent of what you say by the time you walk out the door, be sure to make points visually stimulating and memorable. Get benefits and points into a format people can understand and use in their lives and business.

Old Fashioned Flip Charts

Dare to be different. The reason presenters use old-fashioned flip charts is they are able to make points that do not distract from the presenter.

Flip Chart Presentations Allow The Presenter To Become The Star

When making presentations with computers, the audience may perceive the knowledge may have come from others. After all, it's a computer-generated presentation.

Using flip charts however, shows you know your stuff. That may be reason enough to get out and buy yourself king size markers and a seminar easel.

A simple flip chart presentation is dramatic because it's real and demonstrates you have the knowledge to present your story. *You don't need many flip charts to make big points.*

Here's a secret to help you remember upcoming points on each chart. Print lightly in pencil at the top of each flip chart the content you will put on that page. No one will know what you have written as people cannot see your notes from more than a few feet away. It's like having a teleprompter. Only you will know what is about to happen.

As a sales presenter your job is to sell. People must like you to buy from you. Smile and make yourself friendly and attractive. Do not overstate and do not over sell. To liven up your presentation, use drama and get people thinking:

Use Real-Life Stories. They Add Emotion And Position Products That People Can See In Their Minds And Remember.

You don't have to be a comedian but you must find a way to use humor or levity in your style. Humor brings affinity. Make fun of *things,* make fun of *yourself* or *situations,* **but never make fun of people.** It will not be funny to put others on the hotplate for a joke or any reason in public unless they are politicians, public people or celebrities.

If you make fun of people, you stand the chance people will not like you because they fear you may make fun of them.

A Winning Sales Presentation

Start with the end in mind, YOU MUST HAVE A SALES GOAL.

A sales presentation is not to inform but to persuade. The idea is to deliver and communicate an entertaining, clear concise presentation that follows an order and leads to taking action. If you do not start with this thinking, you may be setting up a presentation to deliver information and it may not sell anything.

The Presentation Overview:

1. The purpose of a presentation is to persuade.

2. People are overloaded and with data.

3. People have short and selective memories.

4. People will not remember facts as much as perceptions.

5. Use originality.

6. Present a new way of seeing an old view.

7. Prove what you say is true.

Do Not:

1. Restate or reposition views that people already know.

2. Be overly simplistic or canned.

3. Add irrelevant details, useless data or filler information not critical to your presentation.

4. Make it hard to understand.

5. Speak in a boring monotonous voice.

Presentations Need To:

1. Get attention.

2. Be meaningful.

3. Be memorable.

4. Lead to taking action.

Selling and persuading is NOT HARD CLOSING OR HARD SELLING. Focus on what is needed, what your company or service does and why they need you. You must be compelling why they need you NOW.

A presentation needs to be persuasive throughout, not hitting hot points in spurts. Sales presentations should flow and be elegant.

Your Presentation Must Have Flow:

1. An introduction.

2. A Body or Story.

3. A Conclusion.

4. A Close.

Presentations are like making one-on-one sales. Presentations need to fill an expectation and follow a logical order or people will get confused.

The introduction sets the stage; you need to get the attention of the group. Start your presentation by telling your audience what they are about to hear and why you are making the presentation in a professional opening.

Let them know what is coming and why. People are smart and they may be thinking they are one-step ahead of you and they know what you are about to present. You must tell them why your presentation will be unique, competitive and the time they spend with you will be well spent.

The body or sales story of your presentation is the why, the need, the benefits of your company or service and why they need you now. Be compelling, persuasive and be professional. Allow people to have fun; you should be enjoying your presentation.

Get feedback. Do not answer questions until you are sure you understand what is being asked. Allow people to visualize the benefits how things will work and what will happen. Draw pictures in their minds and remember that you must reach people both literally and creatively. People learn and digest information differently; cover all the bases of persuasion.

Print your key points before the presentation as handouts. Tell the audience they don't have to take notes and to sit back, enjoy and listen to your ideas.

In Conclusion

The conclusion is not the close. The conclusion is the wrap-up of your presentation. You hit all your points once again in a concise finish that sums up why you are the person they want to deal with and why your product and service is the best.

The close comes last and is a next logical step in your persuasive presentation. If you have set up your presentation and made it properly, closing will be natural. Because you have been persuasive all through the presentation, *asking customers to take action will be expected*. Be specific about what you want.

Close The Sale

Create A Powerful Presence

Distinguish yourself from the competition and provide sales leadership and not "me too" copycat selling. Features, benefits, value and essential information may build a compelling case, but being informative does not move people to take action.

Giving a presentation and public speaking has another physical side: speaking. The more comfortable you are with your skills, the better you present your ideas.

The following speaking tips will help make your points like a professional and keep you looking sharp. Creating a powerful presence is more than presentation skills; it is how you show up. It is not about how attractive you are but about how comfortable you are with yourself. Sellers with a strong presence do not mind being noticed.

When you are presenting, you want to have a powerful presence and portray confidence.

Professional Speaking Tips:

1. **Prepare – Rehearse.** There is no such thing as a good presentation shot from the mouth.

2. **Know Your Audience.** Know what they expect. Research every group you address.

3. **Don't Read.** Use notes to help remind you.

4. **Facial Expression.** Maintain eye contact, look at your audience with a relaxed face and smile.

5. **Appear Natural.** Do not stand behind a podium, it will make you look unnatural and appear stiff.

6. **Movement.** Move with a purpose and on purpose. Use a presidential walk with your head up, shoulders back and don't feel uncomfortable being noticed.

7. **Posture**. A strong posture gives you power. Standing or sitting, position yourself right, shoulders back and head straight.

8. **Eliminate Jargon And Corporate Lingo**. Speak in simple terms, throw out "Selling" language and use your own natural style.

9. **Slow Down.** Speak at a moderate pace with distinction, enunciate carefully, choose words and don't repeat things.

10. **Be Passionate.** Don't get so excited and emotional you do not sell your ideas.

11. **Get Feedback**. People like to be active. Ask questions and keep the audience involved.

12. **Share A Story**. "Hook" the audience with a story to get attention, inspire or move people.

13. Audiences Sense Fear. Be sure they feel your confidence.

People may not remember data. However, **they will remember how you touch them and make them feel**. This is the key to public speaking and making great presentations that will have people talking.

Elevator Pitching

The elevator pitch is named because it should last no longer than the average elevator ride. You never know when you will meet new prospects so you must be prepared to get attention quickly and not fumble opportunity.

Create The Elevator Pitch To:

- **Sell yourself in *your own style***

- **Sell your story persuasively in one minute**

Few salespeople and executives pay attention to this basic skill or why it's important. An elevator pitch may give you an opportunity to tell others about you and your product that otherwise may never happen.

Be prepared with a minimum of three important points about your company or service that sets it apart. Your goal is to create a great first impression good enough to get you a second meeting. You must be prepared to get your ideas and pitch across before a potential client or customer disappears on you.

The following points are a guide as you prepare your pitch. Choose only key points that will spark interest and be persuasive in 60 seconds or less. Practice and read the pitch aloud:

1. What is the idea?

2. What is the market?

3. What are the benefits?

4. Who are the competitors?

5. Is your product or service a brand?

6. What key points do you tell and what do you leave out?

7. What do you change for your specific audience?

Keep your ideas fresh and leading edge. Once you get an elevator pitch down, you will not be caught off guard or at a loss for words at a critical opportunity.

Delivering important information in a short time takes strategic thinking and planning. The tendency is to overload others with data and that is exactly what you *do not* want to do.

What you say can spark interest or bore people. What you highlight will get others to ask questions or turn them off. No matter what you sell, what works in print or online may not work in a quick pitch so you may need fresh thinking to create an inspiring elevator pitch.

I See All Of You

People who create good impressions and present themselves well receive preferential treatment in virtually every area of life. It's your overall impression that defines you and helps create the image you can be trusted.

Even if your appearance is not the most important thing to you, *it is important to people you meet and sell.*

People Are Visual, We Are Judged In About Two Seconds Flat

Business associates are going to judge you by your attire. Studies show that for better or worse, shaking off a bad first impression seldom changes. You cannot change how people think however; you can change their impression of you.

When dressing for business or business casual, take time to educate yourself. You don't have to spend a fortune to dress well but here is a tip from my years in the fashion business:

- **Accessories Set Up Your Look And Highlight Your Clothing**

- **How Well Clothes Fit Is As Important As How Much You Spend On Them**

If you are on a budget, spend the key money on accessories and find a good tailor. Buy fewer clothes but buy better clothes. Quality fabrics and shoes last longer and look better. Buy good shirts that fit well, buy good ties. Matching your accessories will allow average suits and skirts to look better. Keep shoes polished and looking fresh.

Regardless of what colors you choose, be sure they compliment and flatter your features. Flashy necklaces may detract from a professional appearance and oversize earrings will not likely compliment the rest of your wardrobe.

Few people know what suits or outfits cost. However, if clothing does not fit well or the accessories do not match, no matter what you spend, you will never look your best.

As a rule of thumb, dress as well or better than people you are doing business with. If you are in the creative field, you have more leeway but you still have to keep in mind the company you are representing. Overall, the goal is simple: *look better than anyone else.*

If you do not have a flair or knack how to prepare your wardrobe, get someone with experience to help you. Do not underestimate how important it is that you:

Look Like a Leader

The Power Of Brilliance

Twenty-five hundred years ago, Sun Tzu, the Chinese war strategist wrote the "Art of War" and the work is still a contemporary tool. Legend is Napoleon studied the work and claimed it the key to victories in Europe. Rommel studied it in North Africa and Lee Iacocca read the strategies to help him accomplish success.

> *Now the general who wins a battle makes many calculations in his temple before the battle is fought. The general who loses a battle makes but few calculations beforehand.*
>
> **—Sun Tzu**

The words are old but the idea is not. Sales presentations give you tremendous opportunity to show your personal talents as well as sell your product or service.

Lazy sellers look for an easy way out by not taking the time necessary to do a complete and through. They use bits and pieces of old presentations to put a pitch together.

Be willing to prepare. Treat opportunities individually and you will win more often. Preparation is the key to professional presenting.

How You
Think Is Everything

- The Will To Win Is The Will To Prepare
- A Sales Presentation Is To Persuade People To Take Action
- Dress Like A Leader, Look Great
- The Secret Is Not Making Lots Of Presentations, It's Presenting Well And Making Sales
- Have An Elevator Pitch Ready To Go At All Times
- Make Your Presentations Original, Exciting And Find A New Way Of Seeing Old Viewpoints
- People Buy From Who They Like—Be Nice, Be Friendly, Smile And Have Fun

CHAPTER 9

Closing The Door On Old School Closing

People don't appreciate old school closing techniques of the past generations. We have a hangover of sales tactics from the days of a high demand and low supply economy.

Consumers and buyers are in control and this is far different than previous generations. People are taking advantage of increasing supply as the internet, computers, software and productivity drive competition.

The marketplace has changed how products are bought and sold. Over decades, companies have spent billions of dollars designing sales strategies and systems to educate customers on their products and company. However, many of those strategies will work only as long as it's a seller-controlled marketplace.

Even though our population has grown and demand has increased, bigger companies and a larger marketplace have not moved faster than innovation, technology and productively. In spite of more demands, we have even more goods and supply. Now customers are in the stronger position and dictate many selling strategies. Companies must pay attention to changing trends or be left behind.

The internet is largely responsible for educating consumers and buyers. What worked like a charm in the 1970s, 80s and 90s is not charming people in today's new economy. Products are bought and sold in an open marketplace thanks to massive changes and improvements in communication.

ABCs Of Closing Are Closed Out

The ABCs "Always be closing" hardball is well known. People see it coming a mile away. Executives especially do not like to be hard-closed and will treat strong-arm hard sales tactics right out the door.

People simply do not want to deal with product pushers and they do not have to. Selling what you have, not what people need is old news and people are on to that game. Not differentiating yourself and your offering based upon unique values will get you a resounding, "No thanks" and "Do not come back."

Closing is nowhere near as difficult as books and gurus make it out to be in the new way of selling. If you cannot close effectively, the problem may have little to do with closing skills and everything to do with your sales tactics.

The Sales Environment Has Changed

Today, salespeople are facilitators. Both the selling and buying process determine if it makes sense to do business together. It does not matter if you are representing a company or an independent agent. The sales person's job is to compare wants, needs and desires of the buyer with what they are selling.

If there is synergy, you may be able to do business and make sales. Qualifying becomes even more important. Otherwise, selling regresses back to simply applying pressure techniques and keeping fingers crossed.

Finger crossing has not proven to be a strong closing strategy although it's a common approach.

The Sales Process—Getting To The Sale

1. **Qualify.** Is your prospect right for your product and are you selling people who can make a buying decision?

2. **Meeting The Customers.** Have you met with the client face to face or on the phone if appropriate? Do the conditions warrant a buying decision?

3. **Selling The Customer.** Have you been able to meet the buyers' needs to bring expected results? Are able to offer the right result for the right price? Is the time right to buy?

4. **Service The Customer.** Give customers what they want and close the sale.

Don't lose track of the big picture. If you cannot close orders, you cannot stay in sales. You simply can't "ask for the business" as a closing technique, that is old school. Set up the sale, present brilliantly like a pro, be sure you have a real prospect and *not a suspect*. If everything lines up, it may be time to try to close the deal.

How To Get To The Close

1. Find out what people want

2. Go and get it

3. Give it to them

4. Get the order

This is how you close sales. *No short cuts.* Do not try to close before it is time. Never forget to ask for the order. If you do your work right, closing will be a pleasant experience:

The Close Is Simply The Act Of *"Making Arrangements"* To Deliver

When you are at the point of closing the sale, *there is no script that will work all the time.* However, there are *sales principles* you follow to improve your sales closing ratio.

Ka-Ching

Closing is not talking as much as it is recognizing buying signals. People tell you they are ready to buy but many sellers pass up an easy close because they are too busy talking and not listening for closing clues.

When prospects ask or question the following, they may be ready to take action. You need to stop selling. It's time to close the order when you hear prospects:

1. Ask about your company or how long has it been in business.

2. How long will delivery take?

3. How much time will it take to install the software?

4. How much training is involved?

5. How can a discount be earned?

6. How much does it cost and what are payment terms?

7. How long is the warranty?

The list of buying questions is endless but the pattern is the same. Once a client starts asking questions that are specific to time, delivery, product, warranty or asks for references, you are in the closing zone.

If you go past this point, you may oversell and miss the close. The next part of the sale takes practice. Short of using duct tape to keep your mouth from killing your sale:

JUST SHUT UP!

I have seen great sellers miss opportunities because they had to close, and close, and close, and close some more. There comes a point when more selling and adding more ideas will only hurt the opportunity to close the order. Simply take the order and thank the customer.

Let Your Sale Be
Something The Prospect Buys
Not Something That You Sell

All you have to do is say, "Great!" and thank them for the business.

The best close is simply timing after you have done the job of setting up the sale. Only three words are needed to make the day, "I'll take it."

The real sales work is before you close, not the close itself. The best close is simple words and honesty. Stay away from old tricks and set ups that smell of sales baloney and tired tactics.

The Closing Rule:

If You Have Heard The Name Of The Close, *Don't Use It*

The cute ones are the worst like "the puppy dog close" where you offer to leave your product or service and pick it up next week with fingers crossed the customer will not want to give it back.

Sometimes We Win, Sometimes We Learn

Even good salespeople don't close all the time and it has little to do with poor closing strategies, it has everything to do with reasons we have all been guilty of. The following reasons and mistakes may be getting in your way of sales success and stopping you from being a good closer.

Six Reasons The Sale Did Not Close:

1. **Salespeople fear rejection and are afraid to hear "No" so they do not try to close orders.** A critical reason people fail at selling: fear of rejection. Salespeople must not let a timid ego get in the way of the selling process and take rejection personally.

   It is an accepted fact 80 percent of all sales calls end with no. People you call on may not be qualified prospects and that is the job of the seller to find out. Many do not need the product or want it. Others cannot use it. Some will not be able to afford it. There are many reasons people will not buy from you and the least of which may be simply, they do not like you.

   If you are in the selling game and you fear rejection, you need to consider a new line of work. Dealing with "No" is part of sales.

2. **Clients fear failure.** The subconscious fear in the mind of the customer is the greatest single obstacle to making a buying decision. Clients fear:

   1. Paying too much

   2. Buying the wrong product

   3. Making a mistake

   4. Having their boss criticize them

5. Being disappointed with the service or product,

6. The service will not be good enough

The prospects fear's of making a mistake and failing holds people back more than any other single event in the selling process.

3. The buyer does not trust you. The buyer does not trust you is a virtual 99.9% guarantee you will not close the deal. If you are not trusted, you bring little value and you will not be able to build rapport. One of the fastest ways to run your fingernails on the blackboard is to try to close a sale before you should. Try to close before you have sold the prospect and you lose credibility. Trust is what others see in your behavior, not just what you say. Trust and building relationships takes time. As a seller, it's up to you to prove your competence.

4. Focusing on selling and not on helping. In a supply driven marketplace, there may be little reason for people to buy your product or they may not buy at all. If you are selling more than being a problem solver and helper, it may likely backfire on you. The overwhelming amount of your time should be spent serving and helping, not selling. Selling is the easiest part and a no-brainer. Problem solving and asking the right questions to get to solutions is the hard part.

5. You're from Venus and they are from Mars. If you are trying to close with yesterday's one-liners and closing strategies, you may as well be on a different planet. People are smarter, enlightened and your best bet and safest play is do not try to use outdated tactics that clients probably know better than you do. Build relationships, present brilliantly, gain trust, add value. Remember that *sales tactics build resistance, not relationships.*

6. **You're off target; you didn't listen.** You must be in tune. What you're selling and what people want may be two different things. People often buy what they want over what may be obvious or what may be needed. A sale may be lost because sellers focus on selling and not listening.

Your Job Is Not To Judge Others, It's To Help and Profit From Them

Prospects will tell you all you need to know if you listen more than you speak.

Why Books, Workshops, Training And Sales Managers Laser Focus On Closing

Why isn't the success rate higher for new salespeople? It's a paradox. Many come into sales and do not get up to speed fast enough. One of the realities sellers face is not enough time to get experience. If they do not make sales, they may never get the chance to move ahead and perfect the necessary skills to master the game.

While you must be patient enough to learn skills, *you must be patient in a hurry.* Learning how to sell takes a sense of urgency. Like any trade or specialized skill, it takes time to learn the ropes. However, in learning how to sell, you may not have the luxury of time.

Learning sales skills is not enough; you must be able to perform the skills. Sellers are on the hot seat to prove they can actually sell and close orders. If you cannot make sales, your potential will dry up in short order.

Getting started in sales is like a new draft starting at a professional football training camp. The new draft knows it will take time to develop skills. However, if they do not throw themselves into the game and prove themselves quickly they may not get a chance to stay on the team.

People earn four to seven-year degrees in higher learning institutions to become professionals, such as doctors, accountants and attorneys. Yet salespeople are expected to be performers in just a few weeks or months of education. To understand the situation, you have to appreciate that there is a huge reality gap between what salespeople learn and what they really need to know to make a living.

Beg
For Forgiveness

So while professionals make closing easy, if you are new to selling, get yourself bloody. Learn how to ask for orders at every opportunity so you can master the technique or you will not make it through the first draft. Just do it and if you make a mistake, *beg for forgiveness.* If you don't do it there will be nothing to forgive, you will be gone. Learning how to sell and close orders takes more than education, it takes:

Acts Of Commission, Not Omission

Closing A Cool Glass Of Water

When I was in high school, a Fuller Brush salesman let me work under him. I was too young to get a sales job on my own so he agreed to pay me a part of his commission on every sale I could make. At the time, I was making my lunch money cutting lawns in the summer heat of Miami so I was up for anything to get out of the heat.

This sales job only required a short sleeve white shirt and a clip on black tie. I had to go door to door, give away free potato scrubbers and ask if I could come in and show them sales samples.

I had the right attitude, no experience and absolutely no sales savvy. However, I also had no preconceived notions and I remember my sales boss telling me,

"Don't worry, if people don't buy, it's not personal. Just go next door and try again."

I didn't let rejection bother me, I was told to expect it. I was like a wooden soldier marching door to door and soon enough I began to figure out what I said that people liked.

If someone said no thanks after they let me in to show them samples, I thanked them for letting me come out of the heat. I would ask for a glass of water. Asking for a glass of water was what got me sales. It was a closing tool I discovered by accident.

It helped people realize I was just a high school kid selling brushes in the heat of summer door to door. I usually got orders from people who had said no thanks. However, after I got that drink of water, the sale was back in high gear and it usually began with the housewife asking, "Let me see the oven brush again," or something like that.

Of course, they felt sorry for me. That was why I was able to sell brushes. I felt that they did need new brushes and mops. What I was selling was better than the old stuff people had in their kitchen and bathroom drawers.

I sold brushes like crazy and when people said "No", they were not saying "No" to me personally, they were simply saying, no thanks, we don't need anything. I was learning an important lesson:

You Need To Develop Thick Skin In Order To Brush Off Rejection And Move On

Many sellers fail because they take rejection personally when it's simply a part of the sales profession. Selling brushes or hundreds of thousands of dollars in advertising is the same principle: do your best to help others but be prepared, you cannot sell everyone.

Selling is a process that leads to an end. Your job is to close the deal. The more you master the basics and set up the close, the better your closing ratio.

Selling is about persuasion, influencing others and getting people to take action. The secret to getting people to move on decisions is easy enough to learn but not simple to execute. That's why so many sellers never achieve more than mediocrity. They underestimate the importance of doing the basics brilliantly and don't focus on doing first things first.

Master setting up the close to win more often.

Be A Good Closer
Or
Get To Be A Good Closer

How You Think Is Everything

- The Sales Environment Is Supply Driven And Customers Are In Control

- Selling Is A Process; Salespeople Are Facilitators And Persuaders

- Closing Is One Tactic Of Sales Strategy

- Don't Judge Others; Help Them And Profit From It

- Ask Questions And Be An Active Listener To Pick Up Closing Clues

- Fear Of Making A Mistake Is The #1 Reason Buyers Won't Buy

- Fear Of Rejection And Not Asking For The Order Is The #1 Reason Salespeople Fail

CHAPTER 10

Will the Real Objection Please Stand Up?

Subconscious fear in the mind of the prospect may be the greatest single obstacle to taking action or making a buying decision. They fear they may be making a mistake, paying too much, buying the wrong product or they will be criticized.

We have an inbred condition and resistance to buying things because of the possibility they may not work out. In addition, we have a history and perception of an adversarial relationship with the selling process. Buyers do not want to be gamed while salespeople are saying how dare those clients "object" to our great presentations.

If you are not selling up to expectations, it may have more to do with your attitude and how you approach people than you realize. If you are not a successful seller, buyers and customers are certainly handing it back to you!

Either you are a catalyst in making the sale or you are a bottleneck in the sales process. You want to be the one ingredient clients and customers cannot do without. Be indispensable. There are many companies throwing sales reps at so many businesses today that you need to do things to stand out.

How Prospects See Things

Buying is an important function in both big and small companies. Buyers learn how to deal with sales reps. Salespeople may have to sell and negotiate with people who appear to have little or no interest in their product. Focusing specifically on price is one tactic in the strategy how buyers handle salespeople.

This is no surprise considering over fifty percent of training for purchasing managers is negotiating and communicating. Over the years, buyers have seen it all. As long as prospects feel sellers have little concern other than to make a sale, a natural defense mechanism takes over.

Customers are cautious until they can determine the truth. They might need or want a product or service but they do not trust or want to do business with you for any number of reasons.

Eighty percent of the time salespeople will meet the same answer, "No." Sales objections are a normal part of the selling process. New and inexperienced salespeople fear an objection because it is rejection.

Pros Look For NOs

Professionals and experienced salespeople know objections help make sales. Objections show interest. They enable salespeople to give more information to the prospect.

The more information the prospect has, the easier it is to make the sale. Objections are part of the process which results in prospects getting information to help make buying decisions. What buyers and customers are *objecting to is the question.* You must get past the smoke screens.

The needs/satisfaction system of selling has been around for generations and for many continues to work as a key selling tactic. However, more and more, that pitch is not working.

Buyers and customers *are not all thinking alike.* The sales process changes; it's a paradigm shift. It has everything to do with a new generation of thinking, a different economy and increased competition.

Old School Selling Needs/Satisfaction

The needs/satisfaction selling process is that a sales person goes in to ask questions to find out what the needs are. This assumption is that *needs actually matter* and the customer actually *knows what they want.*

Sellers find out what the needs are and based on those needs, put a pitch, proposal or presentation together. This will usually lead to objections: too fat, too thin, too big, too small, too expensive, lousy value, not fast enough, too slow or simply I don't like it because it's the wrong color.

It is a sales game and everyone knows it. It is not as if this process is a real authentic conversation on either side. The salesperson has the intent to sell and get the buyer to buy and both sides know it.

This system based on simple left-brain logical need draws the conclusion that people make decisions based on what they need. That is simply not true. When it comes to taking action and making buying decisions, you can bet the decisions will be emotional and win over intellect and logic virtually every time.

You only have to look to yourself as an example. You may have needed a new wardrobe for the job but if you wanted a new car, you bought the new car. The wardrobe can wait. We all experience knowing what we need **but doing what we want.**

You cannot assume the prospect can actually tell a seller what the needs are. The problem is the emotional wants may not be on the surface of the buyer's mind but beneath the surface. People simply do NOT know what they need much less what they want.

Change your thinking and CHANGE YOUR ATTITUDE. All things will change if you fundamentally change your philosophy. The customer is not a convenient money flow pipeline directly to your wallet simply because you are selling something, selling is not *conquering people.*

Your responsibility is to serve others, not to have all the answers; no one does. Do not assume anything and you will earn respect and build relationships.

Eliminating Objections

1. **People buy both intellectually and emotionally.** Do not focus on needs over wants! If you make assumptions, you may be as wrong as you are right. It's not your job to take that risk. More often than not, people will buy what they want. **Need is WHAT they want, WHY is the emotion behind their action.**

Ask the question **WHY**; it leads to fewer objections and more sales.

2. **The Sales Job Is Not To Judge Others.** It's to help them get what they want or need and make a profit from them.

3. **If the salesperson's intent is simply to sell things, that is a conflict of interest.** Do not put making a sale ahead of customer's needs and wants. The attitude is to help, solve and be collaborative rather than divisive. No one likes to be had; no one likes to be gamed and people hate to be sold. If people distrust your intentions and do not trust your honesty, you are not going to be making many sales.

4. **Your product or service is not going to help or be in the best interest of the client.** *Getting the sale at any cost will be costly.* If your prospect is not really a candidate to buy, thank them for their time and move on to the next sales opportunity. Tell the client what you are really thinking and offer suggestions that may help. Integrity may come back to you later when you do have something that will work for the prospect.

5. **People do not simply buy from people they like.** They buy from people they *like, trust and value* to help solve problems.

It Takes Fresh Eyes To See Old Paradigms

Competition has forced sales management positions to become more administrative. However, as a seller it is not *your* job to administrate but to make things happen. Buyers do not care about your internal company problems or what your company or service cannot do. They want to know what and how things can be done.

Prospects are not the enemy unless you position them to be at war with you. They reflect thinking of the marketplace that may be well ahead of past selling tactics and strategies.

Where Did This Thinking Come From?

At the end of World War II, the world could best be described as one where anyone would buy for any reason. In that age, consumers had been through a long war and an even longer depression and when things started to get better, workers became consumers and the race for new sales strategies and tactics evolved.

People were anxious to buy anything from anyone and they did. That led to selling strategies and practices that are not relevant today. Competition was scarce and people were not as educated and enlightened. The sales game for many became a wham bam and thank you for easy pickings as marketers and companies flourished without a competitive environment.

Today we live with intense competition, worldwide manufacturing and instant communication. It is not only emails and files flying through the internet, it's new ideas and innovations.

We have many more choices and improved quality of products and services than in the past. Technology, communication, education and knowledge have changed our business models and our society.

Competition has changed the playing field. Treat people like as you would like to be treated. Because you are a seller, career success is even more relevant to your accountability.

Find More Qualified Customers

Many salespeople spend too much time with prospects who "have great potential," but for some reason never seem to buy.

The average and inexperienced salespeople go through all of the motions looking like they are selling, but the scorecard continually shows, **they don't bring in the business.**

Average salespeople qualify prospects and almost never disqualify their prospects. Not knowing how to prospect effectively and efficiently will lead to a lot of wasted time and typically, NO sales.

You have to get real with the fact that not everyone will buy from you; you cannot sell everyone. Objections are part of selling.

However, if your intent and behavior are right, obstacles and objections are not a personal affront or attack on you. You are more likely in control of how many objections you are getting then what your closing radio is.

To increase productivity, increase your personal profitability and earn more sales, develop relationships where you bring value trust and respect.

Most sellers are happy to get along with a buyer or customers and simply getting along will bring average performance. To get a maximum return on your time build real authentic relationships and go from selling to helping and solving.

Sellers deal with objections and that is part of the game. The way to sell more is to be sure your thinking and behavior reflects the times we're in. Do not force unnatural divisive strategies and sales tactics on prospects.

You may be inviting unnecessary objections simply because you are not putting the customer ahead of you.

How You
Think Is Everything

- Fear Of Failure Prevents People From Making Buying Decisions

- To Understand Objections, You Must Understand How Others See Things

- A New Generation Of People Will See The Sales Process Differently

- People Don't Want To Be Sold And People Hate Being Gamed

- People Most Often Buy What They Want Over What They Need

- Add Value, Be Collaborative And Gain Trust

CHAPTER 11

The Competitive Edge: Product Knowledge

Knowing just enough to sell your product is far different from being an expert on your product. After all, isn't that the marketing and engineering department's role? Why not pick up the phone and ask for help?

Yes, you can get by and you can sell with a fair understating of your product. That leads to average. If you want to become more, you have to do more than simply know your product or service.

There is a fine line for sellers on the importance of product knowledge. There is no doubt companies are focused on salespeople learning product knowledge and skills. However, companies do not spend enough time and effort helping sellers develop their personal skills and presentation ability.

Product knowledge is critical to the sales effort. However, product knowledge for sellers *must be used to help sell products,* not simply try to educate customers. Customers resent salespeople trying to become educators.

Assuming you know more than customers and clients because you have product knowledge may lead you to big sales trouble. Your job is not to educate, it's to use your product knowledge to sell.

The difference of knowing your stuff and being brilliant may only be a tiny edge. It's the same thing as a thoroughbred horse that wins more races. All it takes is a couple of inches ahead at the finish line to win. Often it will come down to your expertise and your product knowledge.

Even if you are in the most conservative company, your function of selling is entrepreneurial. Your success gets measured by results, not how you look, talk or behave. If you have all the attributes of success, but you cannot make the rubber hit the road, you cannot win.

Selling is numbers and it is measurable. You produce or you do not. You must be an authority on the product and the market. You must have sales skills to make things happen.

Product Knowledge Is Your Edge But It Will Not Replace Personal Sales Skills

While the average seller is doing what is asked, they may be doing little more and expecting the company or others to help them. Your edge is to take advantage of human nature. Don't take anything for granted.

In virtually every business, there is more to learn than what is on the surface. When we talk about products and service, it's also the marketing, research, competition and critically, the benefits from what you sell. You must understand everything about what you are presenting.

Where To Start

Your job is to understand prospects and clients so you can help them get what they want. Understanding your buyer will show you have empathy, you are interested in them and what they do. A buyer will appreciate you taking the time to try to understand their needs.

Learn the basics and focus on the fundamentals of what you sell as best as you possibly can. Product knowledge can absolutely make or break a sale. You must be current on your industry and understand the marketplace you sell in.

Sales Begins With Knowing Your Product:

1. **Product Knowledge Affects Sales.** Prospects and clients rely on you to help them make decisions. Understand your unique product strengths and weaknesses in order to help clients and give you an added sales edge.

2. **Product Knowledge Boosts Your Enthusiasm.** Customers and prospects will relate to sellers who know their product well enough to be enthusiastic about the benefits it brings to clients.

3. **Product Knowledge Helps You Become A Better Communicator.** The more you know, the better your ability to present and sell.

4. **Product Knowledge Allows You To Answer And Field Questions.** No one you sell to should know more about your product than you. Customers expect you to be the expert in your field as well as your product. Knowing your product inside and out helps you determine how to fit customer needs and field questions.

5. **Product Knowledge Leads To Trust And Confidence.** *Product Knowledge is Sales Power.* It is much easier to build a relationship once prospects and customers trust your expertise and knowledge.

Advertising And Marketing Influences Buying Decisions

Marketing has one prime purpose, to sell things. Marketing creates awareness and helps create a perception to stimulate the sales process.

While marketing is non-transactional, you must be aware of the influences it may have on your buyers and the marketplace.

People perceive your company through experience, advertising, salespeople, tradeshows and marketing. You must be aware of the message your company sends to clients as well as the message your competition is sending. You may also be dealing with a lack of marketing and you as a salesperson may be the head marketing machine.

People are swayed by perceptions. All people have paradigms and see from their own perspective.

We All Filter Information And Make Judgments Not On What Is Real, But What We Perceive To Be Real

Marketers are keenly aware how perception works and play to that strategy. In reality, we all make buying decisions on what *we think* we know to be true.

What You Don't Know Can Hurt You

It is your responsibility to be up to speed on competitive advertising. Any competitive marketing message may influence your clients and that is your concern. Sales won and lost for reasons that may be real or perceived concern you. *What you do not know can hurt your sales.*

Know Your Competition

If you send an unclear message and can't make distinctions that will help accounts become buyers, you are your own competition. You are beating yourself and shooting yourself in the foot.

I sold against supposed sales professionals who could not make a list of their competition or know what distinguished their products. They were easy to beat. The question is, just how well do you know your competition?

Being An Expert On The Competition:

1. Their strengths

2. Their liabilities (all competitors have them and so do you)

3. How they do business, present their product and make sales

4. Their complete product or service

5. Their pricing and how they package themselves

If you are selling and don't have these key areas covered, it would be like a politician trying to get votes but not watching the polls to see what was swaying voters.

How can you sell your product and unique benefits effectively if you do not understand how your buyers and clients are making distinctions? What your competition says is your business.

You must be able to articulate uniqueness and what you do in a special way or you will be a common commodity. If you are a commodity, your value is less and you are relegated to selling on price alone.

What To Sell, When And To Whom

Companies spend billions of dollars inundating customers and clients with marketing and advertising.

To make decisions how to better sell things, companies use computers and sales data to track what customers buy and how often. It enables target marketing, data mining and focused advertising.

However, tracking history and making projections about what customers will do barely earns a sixty percent success rate. That is hardly better than a coin toss of fifty percent. Numbers give you history but *history will not predict the future.* History guides you to indications of what may happen.

Companies miss the target more often than not. You must be on top of your competition and changes to keep that product knowledge edge. That edge is both what you sell and what is happening in the marketplace.

Taking a shot at competitors is not smart selling and often bad business. Buyers and customers resent direct competitive mud throwing. You need to know about what others sell to POSITION YOUR PROUDCT OR SERVICE TO BE SOLD IN THE BEST POSSIBLE WAY.

Use competitive information to steer away from potholes and land mines and laser focus on benefits. Product knowledge means product, both your and competitors. Don't get blind-sided by lack of understanding and information. As a seller, you are the pro.

In fast changing times, you can never get ahead of what will be coming next; product knowledge is a nonstop learning game. Top performance sellers know their products and that knowledge is sales power.

How You
Think Is Everything

- **Product Knowledge Is Selling Power And Your Competitive Edge**

- **Perception Is Reality. Understand The *Perception* Of Your Product Or Service**

- **Advertising And Marketing Of Your Product And Your Competitor Is Your Concern**

- **What You Don't Know About Your Competition Can Hurt You**

- **Stay On Top Of Changes And Don't Assume All The Moves Your Competitors Make Are The Right Moves**

CHAPTER 12

Fill The Sales Funnel, Slow The Attrition

The sales funnel is a visual step by step metaphor of the sales process; it's wide at the top and narrow at the bottom. As you put unqualified prospects in the top of the funnel, what come out the bottom are the qualified leads. These leads become the real potential after you put them through the sales process. The sales funnel is a far better estimator of future sales than keeping a laundry list of unqualified leads.

The sales funnel is also a way to monitor active accounts that drop away over time; it's the law of attrition. In military strategy, attrition is wearing down the enemy by continual losses in personnel and material. In business, customer attrition is the loss of clients or customers.

Nothing Lasts Forever

There are plenty of reasons accounts whither and die. Dissatisfaction with service, technical support, billing disputes, company polices, bankruptcies, takeovers. New people at your accounts may bring in the new suppliers. There are countless reasons accounts churn that have little do with the selling efforts.

The job of sales is to stay ahead of the game by continually selling and adding new accounts. The problem in sales is maintaining a constant flow of revenues and sales every month. Selling rarely moves ahead in a nice even straight line always pointing higher.

Repeatedly, sales fall off followed by sharp increases only to fall down in the following month. The way to lessen the drops and increase sales is to work the sales funnel and keep adding to the list of qualified leads.

The more you have in the funnel, the more reliable your flow of business you have over the year. If you fall down on your prospecting, it's only a matter of time until your sales begin to fall. Attrition and losing accounts is a fact for sellers and universally involuntary.

In almost every case, the lack of new sales and consistent revenues is the failure to prospect and develop new business. You must work the sales system that keeps more accounts working through the sales funnel.

You cannot let your current hot leads, attention demanding prospects or making sales presentations stop your prospecting and lead generating. The time to find new business is when business is hot and things are working well, not when things are slow.

The sales adage may not always be, "There's light at the end of the tunnel." If you don't work your sales system you may discover another sales adage, "It can't get any darker in here," just as the lights go out and you go to total blackness. No one is immune from economic forces;

no one stays even in a competitive world. You must be moving ahead or you will fall behind:

Only the paranoid survive.
—Andrew Grove
Former Chairman, President and CEO
Intel Corporation

When you are in good times and things are rolling along remember eventually you get rain on your parade and it may be a downpour and wash you out.

Don't get cocky and feel attrition will not strike your accounts. It happens when least expected. The last to know a divorce is coming is usually the happy partner blinded by the feeling, *all is going so well.*

Tips To Keep The Sales Funnel Full:

1. **Lower Your Attrition Rate.** It takes a lot more time and energy to sell a new account than it does to "hold on" to an existing satisfied account.

2. **Keep A Close Eye On Your Current Accounts.** Keep customers happy. Stay in touch with notes, emails and phone calls and show up in person on a regular basis.

3. **Improve Your Prospecting And Make Qualified Prospecting Calls.** The more qualified calls you make, the more calls you convert to appointments. Qualified appointments dramatically improve the odds of closing sales.

4. **Increase Your Referral Rate**. Current satisfied accounts are your best source of

referrals. Ask for help. Get referrals and testimonials from current customers.

5. **Go To Trade Shows**. Hand out business cards and meet new people. Join networking groups.

6. **Open A Web Account**. Join a web based online business and social networking site like LinkedIn. Look out for new online networks starting up.

7. **Create An Internet Page.** Sell you and your product online. Create a web page where you can refer accounts and prospects.

8. **Write Articles.** Both print and online publications look for contributions from professionals. Write articles and post them on your websites.

9. **Volunteer To Speak.** Make presentations at trade shows and invite your customers and prospects.

10. **Do Mailings And Invitations.** Database your accounts and prospects. Keep your name in front of people and become a marketing machine.

The sales job is service, adding new accounts and growing the business. Sellers who do not pay attention to attrition will have to work harder. They rarely become top performers. Without attention, even the most loyal accounts can drift away to be rescued by a competitor.

We tend to focus on new business and needlessly neglect current clients because they are not that important or they may leave anyway. This is shortsighted thinking. Pay attention to the *time and effort it took to get new accounts in the first place:*

Keeping Existing Customers Is Far Less Effort than Getting New Ones

Make a distinction between **voluntary churn** that happens to you and **involuntary churn** that you let happen. Companies and sales managers watch attrition because the base revenue of customer accounts is the way you measure a sales system. If sales start to slide, the first question will be, "What happened to our accounts?"

For salespeople, the way to become a top producer is to decrease the attrition rate. If you lose an account and you add one, you are even. If you add an account and you hold on to what you have, you are building your business.

Getting a customer referral is one of the most powerful and often the least used ways to build your business.

In business, there is an important principle that works in virtually every sales situation. If you want more business, add more accounts and profits will rise. However, if you want profits to jump exponentially, reduce expenses at the same time you add more business and the profits go thorough the roof.

Cutting expenses and adding accounts is a business strategy that exponentially increases profits. In sales, do these two things at once to improve performance. Use lead generating time more effectively and sell new accounts at the same time. Do more:

There Is Never Enough Time In The Day For Sellers

When you add up what you have and how much a current billing account is worth, you have to look at how much time it takes to replace accounts.

What is universally hated and old generation strategy is cold calling. It's an inefficient use of time in today's fast moving business economy:

Cold Calling Is Cold Selling

The Cold Numbers:

1. If you cold call 100 people you are lucky to get 15 to 20 appointments.

2. The appointments are COLD, not qualified.

3. You will be lucky to make one sale out of the appointments you get.

4. The odds are 100 to 1. Slot machines pay better odds.

Cold calling is a lead qualifying sales process with a low return on investment exercise. It is not recommended unless sellers gain intense sales training and understand that specialized part of the sales process.

A buyer-driven economy puts cold call sellers at an even bigger disadvantage. In recent years because of time restrictions on everyone, cold calling has become even more of an uphill lead generating strategy. It's not a productive use of seller's time compared to strategic targeted prospecting methods. What worked before does not mean it works in today's new economic times.

Asking sellers to cold call is like asking them to be pallbearers at a funeral and the next hour host the wedding. Paying sellers to cold call compared to the cost of hiring full time lead generating professional people is the real issue.

In sales situations that are dependent on a shotgun approach, it will be far more effective and cost efficient to have a dedicated lead generating system. Cold calling trained professionals set up leads and appointments. This frees sellers from making cold calls.

The Best Sales ROI Is To Get Qualified Leads As Efficiently As Possible In the Hands of Sellers And

Keep Sellers Selling

In business-to-business sales, cold calling is not the way to build business. You simply must find a way to get introductions and qualify your sales calls to be an effective seller. You need to find a way to spend more of your time in front of people who make buying decisions and make that your number one priority.

The problem is time. As a seller, you are short of time. However, don't think the average executive has any more time to spare than you do. The average executive has a time crunch and will not agree to see cold calling salespeople. Executives simply cannot waste time without reason.

The Answer?

The opposite of attrition is *retention*. Every account that buys from you is satisfied enough to buy from you. Your accounts will help you if you ask for help.

Business people know other business people and they all know other customers. Even more important, you never know who knows whom. However, if you do not ask for help, it is an odds on bet; *you are not going to get any.*

Having others refer you is a valuable stamp of approval. Successful experience is priceless when others sell you and your story.

Salespeople miss the 2-foot putts because they are embarrassed, afraid, intimidated and fearful or it never occurred to them that others would be willing to help.

Networking is the key to success in business. When you ask for referrals, it's a natural because others are doing it all the time for themselves. It's an open and accepted business practice. Asking people you do business with to help you network and meet others is a business principle almost all are actively engaged in.

How Do You Ask For Referrals?

The more specific you are, the easier it is to get help. Ask specifically for what you need and it will be easier for someone to say, "Yes, I can do that, let me call them now and set you up with an appointment."

If you are vague in what you want, it is difficult to get help. People may be more than willing to help you but do not assume they know what you need or want. Spell out exactly what you are looking for and ask for it.

Get Out More

Go to meetings and trade shows; take your customers out to have coffee, lunch or dinner if appropriate. Don't be afraid to meet clients socially, they may enjoy your company as much as you enjoy theirs.

How do world-class sellers get to be world-class sellers? Do you think the successful and professionals work 9/5 or 24/7?

People you are doing business with may be the same people who you want to hang out with as well. Business contacts you deal with may be literally the neighbor next door. The difference is:

They Are Already Doing Business With You

Don't overlook your social network of people who can help you with referrals. If you don't network and ask for referrals from accounts, it would be like winning a major league poker game only *you left the pot on the table.*

While you are asking for referrals, ask if you can help your customers and clients, not just to sell them more stuff! Be helpful, be authentic and others will help you.

Make Selling A Team Sport: Play Ball With Customers

Do you know your competition? Are they friendly, can they help you? Can you help them? I found that my competition was willing to share leads and information. Sales competitors are doing what you are doing, selling accounts and customers.

Competitors are not necessarily the enemy; it depends on your industry and your business. Your competitor may have leads and business they cannot handle. For any number of reasons it may be good sales business to share common information and leads for mutual benefit.

Keeping the sales funnel full creates long-term success, lowers the drama and makes the sales game more enjoyable. However, what works today can always work better. Be on the lookout for new ways to birddog and prospect new accounts to build your backlog of potential sales.

Leverage your contacts and base of business to get more business is your secret key to sales success. Meet new people and make it a priority to get referrals. Keeping the sales funnel full is not simply a list of names but a growing list of qualified names that you can turn into customers. The more you use referrals to help you, the more you take advantage of an important edge.

Ask and you shall receive.

An Introduction Is Not Only a Foot in the Door, It's An Invitation to Do Business.

How You Think Is Everything

- **Attrition Is A Universal Involuntary Fact Of Life For Sellers**

- **A Steady Stream Of Referrals Is Key To Improving Sales**

- **Don't Ignore Your Active Customers**

- **Sellers Never Have Enough Time—Don't Waste It On A Poor Prospecting System**

- **Calling On Qualified Prospects Dramatically Improves Sales**

- **Cold Calling Is Simply Not Efficient For The Majority Of Salespeople**

CHAPTER 13

Managing Time And Accounts

There are not enough hours in the day to get things done. Cutting fat from your life will help make the most out of time and energy. Time is our most precious commodity. The better you use your time, the more productive you become.

Self-discipline is the key in top performance selling. Work on critical things to reach goals, not just the urgent things. Use the 80/20 rule and focus on what will make you successful.

You don't need a stethoscope to hear the pulse of successful business people: time is money.

How Salespeople Use Time Will Make Or Break Them

Don't waste time simply prioritizing your daily schedule. **Instead, schedule your priorities.** Get important things done first. Make a distinction between important and urgent or fire drills will eat up your time.

The Pickle Jar Theory Of Prioritizing

One of the best theories for time management is the idea of "fit." You start with a large jar. To effectively fill the jar, put the big rocks in first. Next, add the pebbles and finally, fill the jar with sand. If you have a pickle jar filled with rocks, pebbles and sand, you have effectively filled in the space.

However, if you empty the jar and fill it with the sand first, you will not be able to put all the rocks and pebbles back in the jar.

Effective time management is similar to the pickle jar. Start with the big and critical sales tasks, then work on lesser tasks and finally fill in the day with the least important tasks.

Good Judgment Counts

Salespeople with good judgment develop a high sense of priority. Sellers face countless problems daily. Some problems are huge while many are insignificant details to sift through.

Sorting out the big from the small is no small task. It takes horse sense and that is not a given. Many have no sense or priority and do not have experience to know what is important to focus on.

It has very little to do with intelligence. People who want to succeed in the time-starved game of sales must allocate the time and energy as if they were in their own business.

You must decide what you want and what is important. What sales goals you are working towards? It's not enough to have desire or a good attitude. It takes action. Break things down to bite sized achievable tasks that make it easy to get them started and accomplished. Get in the habit of dropping what is not working and doing more of what is working.

Account Management: Art Or Science?

What keeps salespeople from selling more? They don't spend enough time selling! Twenty-five to thirty-eight percent of salespeople spend time specifically devoted to selling. That translates into the average salesperson spending approximately 19 weeks out of 50 weeks selling. No wonder salespeople feel overwhelmed with other things to do besides selling.

The business of selling has changed. Buyers and consumers are smarter, more enlightened and it has everything to do with competition, education and new technologies. Hand held communicators send notes and information immediately from everywhere. Cell phones have changed the lives of sellers.

Years ago, outside sales was the place to be for big jobs and income. Today inside sales has become equally important. It has everything to do with changes in the way we do business.

Customer Relationship Management Tools

CRM or Customer Relationship Management is a system and methodology. Companies need to share data to be efficient and competitive.

CRM systems help organize information to spot happy and unhappy customers, buying patterns, product purchases, sales performance, generate research and reports.

Systems keep track of emails, faxes and organization. In short, CRM systems help with the #1 reason customers defect to competition: poor service and communication.

The downside of CRM for salespeople is it may slow them down, overload them with data entry and waste valuable hours of sales time. Sellers complain management does not use CRM systems (and many managers secretly are computer illiterate), as much as they talk about using it.

Often top sales producers want no part of the new technology while executives spend millions on hardware, software and automation that gathers dust.

Money Making Software

One of the best applications for computers and salespeople is using computer power to manage account lists and juggle information. If you work a sales territory or in a situation that handles lots of accounts and moving parts, *contact software will help make you money.*

Computers and software answer a problem, not enough time to watch everything and having sales fall through the cracks because they were not followed up.

Use ACT!, Goldmine, Outlook, Palm or any contact and reminder software to help you sell more effectively. Make yourself computer literate enough to run simple follow up software to help you make more sales. Either you learn how to help yourself with a laptop computer or it's yellow pads, #2 pencils and colored post it notes.

Getting Out From Under Email

Email is an amazing boost to productivity. In addition, it's a sinkhole of problems that creates stress, anxiety and may become a time waster. It can be overwhelming to have stacks of emails waiting for you in your in box. You cannot stop the mail, but you can manage to save you time.

Tips To Managing Email Overflow:

1. **If you do not need it, get rid of it.** Trash spam and junk immediately.

2. **Do not store emails in your inbox.** Answer what are necessary and put emails in folders to store. If you need to save emails long term, keep a separate "Saved" folder.

3. **Use email like a file cabinet with folders.** Do not keep stuff everywhere; make folders to hold lists and projects. What has to be done immediately, put on a calendar. Print out a daily or weekly calendar.

4. **Prioritize your email.** Separate high-priority from other emails and get them answered and done immediately. Don't let things stack up. Because something just came in does not mean it comes ahead of what is critical to be done. Sort lists, tasks and high to low priority.

Account Management

Prospecting and selling new accounts is only part of the sales process. Effective management of accounts drives revenue through new and existing accounts.

You need to understand customers' critical needs in order to manage accounts. To keep accounts from going to competitors, manage your time so you are in contact and pay attention to their needs.

Managing accounts is important to keep the sales funnel full. You don't get referrals or testimonials from accounts that are not happy.

Whether you use computers and software as selling and system tools or yellow pads and pencils, the critical problem is the same:

Less Follow Up Equals Fewer Sales

No one wins long term without a good system. All business is a system and you will only be as good as the system you create.

The better you organize yourself and use tools to help you, the more time you devote to developing relationships, selling accounts and closing orders.

Don't let distractions stop you from the obvious. Selling is about solving problems and being with customers and clients. Don't let anything stand in your way and use every tool to help you win. Make more time for selling and your sales will increase. Make technology and software a tool to make you more money.

How You
Think Is Everything

- Time Is The Seller's Most Important Commodity

- Sellers Can't Sell More If They Don't Spend More Time Selling

- Sellers Don't Like Systems That Waste Sales Time

- Get An Assistant, A Laptop Or A Yellow Pad But Be Sure You Have A Great Follow Up System

- Email Is A Productivity Tool—Don't Let It Overwhelm You

- Manage Your Time And Manage Your Accounts Like You Own The Business

CHAPTER 14

SMART Goal Setting

Successful people have one thing in common. They focus on predetermined goals. To be a winner in sales, put goals in writing.

As soon as you put goals in writing, you have joined an elite club. Only three percent of the population sets goals. Salespeople, however, are used to goals. Why? Sales jobs are based on numbers, time and performance. Sellers need goals to track results and remind them of where they need to go.

Successful people use goals as reminders and guidelines. Without goals, we would just drift along. Goal setting is proactive strategy. The successful make things happen and don't wait around for things to simply happen to them with fingers crossed.

People need a map to get to destinations. When you have a map, it's like getting in a car and knowing where you want to go. Without a map, you may end up going around in circles. The same principle applies to how you operate your sales life.

You Cannot Accomplish Great Things If You Don't Know What You Want To Accomplish

Goals are a key ingredient of successful salespeople. Many sellers fail because they have no goals.

Make Goals Visible

You must be specific in your goals or they will not appear real in your mind. You cannot say you just want more money. Exactly how much money do you want? You must be specific how much you want to increase your sales. Simply saying you want more will not be enough to drive you. To express a desire to increase sales, you must know exactly how much you want the increase to be.

You must put goals ahead of money. Money in itself is paper or a statement from a bank or financial account. Do you want a new condominium, a nicer car, an extended vacation or is the money going to get you to retirement faster?

The more specific you make your goals, the better you can see yourself reaching them. How big is that condominium, what kind of car, where is that vacation, how much do you need to retire?

Your goals must be visible enough to see them in your mind. Your imagination translates vision into action and energy.

We think logically with our left-brain. We take action with emotions and our right-brain. We use logic for thinking and information, but our emotions drive us to action.

The principle of imagination and energy when working with your goals trains your thinking to be focused and specific.

Setting Goals The SMART Way

Setting effective goals needs guidelines. If you try to do things that are not specific, can't be measured, are not realistic, don't hit your hot buttons and are not time bound, the odds are, they will not happen.

An effective system is thinking SMART and setting goals to define your thinking. Focus on results and clearly emphasize what you want to happen:

SMART Goals Are:

- **Specific**
- **Measurable**
- **Attainable**
- **Rewarding**
- **Timely**

SMART Goals Answer:

- **What?**
- **Why?**
- **How?**
- **When?**

What are you going to do?
Why are your goals important to you?
How are you going to make things happen?
When will goals be achieved?

You should have short-term goals and long-term projects you want to accomplish. They must be measured in time to be specific. If you can't measure goals you will not be able to manage goals. When you measure things, you can see things happen and you can see things changing.

The reason you put your goals in writing is that it gives you a clear vision and target:

Goals Must Be Measurable, Attainable And Realistic

What drives you ahead or holds you back is your subconscious mind. Make sure goals are high enough. Setting guidelines is necessary for your subconscious mind to accept your goals.

Set realistic goals and raise them as you find success. If you overstretch goals like many books tell you, the odds are you will drop out. Once your subconscious mind figures out you cannot accomplish something, it will move on to new ideas. You cannot win if your subconscious mind is against you; it will sabotage your thinking.

To stay motivated and moving forward every journey starts with a step. You cannot run a 4-minute mile just because you are motivated. That will take time, effort and training.

You are better off with reasonable, achievable goals than setting yourself up for failure and just trying to get close. Goal setting is mind-mapping success, not trapping you to into unfilled commitments and guaranteed failure.

The Dark Side Of Goal Setting

We set our goals for personal reasons. Companies set goals for their reasons. In sales, it's a good idea to have collective reasons.

Goal setting has a dark side and may lead to cheating. When goals are arbitrarily set without regard to realistic accomplishments, people who fall short of goals may do what is necessary to hold on to their job or position.

We have seen plenty of business scandals and executives caught cooking the books to meet financial goals. Salespeople may produce phony sales projections or exaggerate sales to keep from being penalized. College executives exclude students with low scores on standardized tests to keep averages up. Don't put it past sellers to do the same tricks.

If you set goals that are not reasonable, they may become a motivator of unethical behaviors and lead to turnover. Additionally, unreasonable and unfair goal setting may create psychological problems when it forces people to admit failure.

Selling is work measured on performance. Managers who do not play by logical and ethical rules and overstate what cannot be accomplished may be setting up failure before the game even starts.

People don't need extra reasons to fudge numbers and mislead companies. Be sure goals are not creating a breeding ground for unethical behavior.

Share The Goals

When people set goals for you, they are not your goals. When you set goals, they belong to you. One sure-fire way to prevent sales problems: don't set goal's without salespeople's input. Reaching agreement with sellers on goals may be the most important factor in setting the goal to begin with. Goal setting works better when information and strategies are shared with everyone involved or sellers may wind up saying, "Well, I never said I could do that. That was your goal, not mine."

Sometimes, Don't Share Goals

In your personal goal setting, unless someone is critically involved in reaching your goal(s), it may not be a good idea to share your goals with others. Negative people, friends, family and neighbors can drag you down in a hurry. Be selective who you share your personal information with. They may be jealous and not supportive.

It's hard enough to keep yourself motivated and focused. Dealing with people who may not be motivated and have no idea what a success track looks like may lead to frustration.

Goals Are Not Bragging Rights

In reality, few people set goals; this is not a popular activity. Goals are not set to be bragging rights; they are set to help you achieve your wants and needs. The best goal is the one you reach, not just talk about.

Review your goals often enough to become part of your routine. Visualize your goal actually completed and keep your subconscious and unconscious minds working towards the goal. Stay away from negative people and replace them with positive self-talk. Hang out with positive, successful people so their attitude and energy rub off on you.

When you make important decisions that affect your time and energy ask yourself, "Does it get me closer to my goal or am I moving in the wrong direction."

The answer is, stay focused and motivated on what will make you win. Your goals must be SMART and in writing. Every decision that gets you *closer to* is the right decision for you. Anything that takes you away from your goals or *further from* is not what you want to do.

Be proactive. Put your goals in writing. It's a habit of leaders and the successful. Put your goals on post it notes and stick them on the refrigerator or bathroom mirror. Remind yourself you are a winner every day and follow your goals to success.

How You
Think Is Everything

- Top Performers Set Goals

- Put Your Goals In Writing

- Setting Unattainable Goals May Be Setting You Up For Failure

- Goals Must Be Achievable And Measurable

- Don't Share Goals With Just Anyone, Be Sure Others Are Positive Thinkers And Will Support You

- Goals Must Be SMART

- Goals Are Not Bragging Rights

CHAPTER 15

A Little Help From The Management

McDonald's is the most successful hamburger seller in the world. So how it is that almost anyone can make a hamburger as good or even better on their backyard grill? The reason McDonald's is a billion dollar leader in the restaurant business is they know how to run a hamburger stand better than anyone does. *McDonald's is a company of brilliant systems!*

Systems Drive Sales

Companies and industries are different, salespeople are different and systems are different. While many things *in* sales and systems are similar, the devil is in the details.

Because you have success in one business does not mean the skills and knowledge will transfer to another business.

If you want top performance, you need top performance strategies. If you treat and train sellers to be obedient and simply follow instructions, you wind up with average performance and your superstar potential sellers are likely to be saved by competitors.

Top performance sellers are likely to be strong willed, independent, creative and will push back when pushed. You must lead people and create an environment that will let them win.

Managers Can't Motivate Others To Do Anything!

People motivate themselves. Managers do not light a fire under salespeople. They give them lighter fluid, matches, wood and a loud music system. People light a fire under themselves for their reasons. The job of management is to find out what motivates people!

Interviewing Salespeople Takes Insight

Hiring right is one of the most important things in sales management. Why are top sellers different? Why do such a small percentage of sellers produce most of the sales? How can sales managers do a better job and not get fooled interviewing?

When hiring sellers, which choices are more likely to be the most effective:

1. **Hiring people with specialized technical experience and training them to be sellers?**

2. **Hiring people with a sales attitude and train them in product knowledge?**

The answer in almost every case is hiring someone with sales aptitude and attitude. You assume you can teach average people to do just about anything and be reasonably competent. Educating and training on the job is rarely that difficult but finding talented salespeople is the real problem for companies and sales managers.

Talented salespeople are harder to find then good technicians because they are in short supply. There are far more educated people with technical aptitude than people with genuine sales skills and ability.

Sizing up behavior how a seller would perform on the job is difficult. How tough are people emotionally? How much rejection can they take before they either give up or learn new skills to overcome rejections? How focused are people and are they able to stay on track over time? What are the unique talents that will make the long-term difference?

I first tried to hire salespeople with my own success traits and quickly discovered that was not a good strategy. People are unique. Stereotyping salespeople leads to hiring mistakes.

Look not only at what you can teach people to do, look at who the people are before you hire them. If their core values are right, the chances of a hiring success increase dramatically. Look for:

Skill Qualities:

1. Personal and Interpersonal Skills

2. Personal Accountability

Attitude Qualities:

1. The 3 Ds: Drive-Determination-Desire

2. Be Continuous Learners

3. Persistence and Resiliency

The tendency is to measure, focus and look for weakness in order to avoid hiring mistakes. *That may lead to hiring average people, which is the opposite of what you are recruiting.* What you should be looking for is balance but most importantly:

Find Strengths *In* People

Trying to find a perfect fit for sales positions may lead to knocking out great candidates. Top performance sellers are not perfect and have flaws like everyone else; they just have *more of the right stuff.* Be sure you are not overcritical of small details that detract you from the important hiring criteria.

The best people I hired had little common demographics. They were younger, older, male, female, short, tall, skinny and overweight. However, none of those traits were able to predict more than average selling performance.

You cannot manage what people say they do, you can only manage behavior. The answer is do your very best to hire the very best and once you make a hiring decision, it's all about behavior. If people do not work out as planned:

Cut Losses Quickly And Move On

Do everything possible to help make new sellers successful. Create a starting environment that fires people up and you wind up managing winners and insure that you made a good hire.

Hiring is a learned skill you develop after years of experience. I never found shortcuts and I do not see any now. Look at interviewing strategies to get better results.

Why Salespeople Love To Hate Sales Meetings

Meetings that are not prepared or simply early morning shakeouts will not inspire or lead to more effective selling. However, if meetings are informative, helpful and lead to more sales, salespeople would look forward to them.

Don't hold alarm clock sales meetings to be sure people are out of bed early. Tell people what time the day starts and hold them accountable. Meetings should help sellers reach their goals, give company and product information and help you as a sales manager reach your goals:

1. **A disorganized sales meeting** is a waste of time for everyone.

2. **Never dress down an individual** seller in front of others for any reason.

3. **Do not let meetings run over 45 minutes.** If you must have long meetings, be sure to break every 50 minutes and tell people that a break will be coming up or they will be hitting the cell phones under the table.

4. **Invite accounts, professionals and company executives** to speak every third meeting. Shake it up, change the meeting place to hotels, client's offices. Make meetings fun and unpredictable.

5. **Instead of reviewing all the sales deals in the hopper,** have people discuss a problem sale then get feedback from the other salespeople how they would approach it.

6. **Have meetings on Monday, not Friday.** Do not play President of the Universe with other people's time. Friday is the END of the week, not the beginning.

The Role of Role-Play

Salespeople may not like to role-play but it may be the best way to improve personal sales performance. Role-playing helps sellers for the same reason professional speakers, presenters and actors rehearse on tape. Role-playing gives important feedback of what works and what does not work.

If you do not role-play, clients and customers are unlikely to tell salespeople they are making speaking or presenting mistakes. They just will not buy from them because they feel the salesperson may be a representation of the product and not up to par.

Role-playing is a great way to try out new ideas, presentations and get feedback in an atmosphere of helpful people. The more salespeople role-play, the more attention it gives to performing and lowers the resistance to presenting in front of an audience.

It's a good idea to video record so people can review their performance in addition to the feedback they get from others.

Role-play may be a separate meeting agenda or it may be part of sales meetings but it should be a regular event.

Sales Teams Are About Individuals

Football is a team game. Selling is a golf game. Sales team camaraderie is great for moral and exchanging ideas but selling is a game of individual performance.

Putting a bunch of assertive, independent personalities together is like a team of horses pulling a wagon. The weak horses may slack off and get a free ride while the strong horses complain they are pulling most of the weight. In time, the strong horses settle down to average if you coral them with average.

All sellers should have regular individual attention and support. Salespeople work together but must be individually recognized based on performance. What gets measured gets done. If you measure a group, you will be missing individual performance.

Yes, Go See The Customers

Sales managers should have relationships with customers. Company executives also should have relationships with customers in their area of responsibility. As the boss and part of the management team, you are perceived to have more power and influence than a salesperson.

It's good business and good for relationships to let customers know they have access to higher levels in a company they are dealing with. Accounts that are important enough to have people from the company call on them directly will appreciate the attention. It helps the sellers as well.

Who Collects?

You don't want to turn salespeople into collection agents. Salespeople are not the most effective way to get accounts to pay up or be timely. However, salespeople have a responsibility to help collections; they sold the account and know the people.

Make sure things start out on the right foot with a good collection agent or department. They have the responsibility to ascertain the credit ability and get that information to sellers and management with specific and timely information.

Many collection problems would never have happened if accounts with lousy credit were not extended credit.

A sale is never compete until the money is collected. Sellers need to be involved with collections but not as the sole collection agent.

Commission plans that pay salespeople in advance of delivery or payment must have rules so sellers know when there is a possibility of losing commissions or getting charged back.

It is not good strategy to take back sales commission from sellers without advance notice. Sellers and specifically 100 percent commission sellers must be involved in the collection effort. Ultimately, collection and commission decisions are up to management.

In the absence of good collection and credit rules, **people will make new rules and justify them**. Developing a good set of credit standards before credit is extended will end needless problems.

Commissions And Salespeople

A sales force paid 100 percent commissions may lead to a conflict of interest.

Asking salespeople on straight commissions to do anything that does not lead to making money in short order will probably not get done in short order, if at all.

However, if the company goal is to add new accounts, that may not be fine for sellers. You may get salespeople to agree in principle but they will focus on the path of least resistance and the most commissions. If it pays more to work with current accounts, sellers will cater to current accounts.

The assumption is 100 percent commission compensation programs will be a motivator for salespeople to work harder. That will not be true in all cases.

Many salespeople will work up to an income level where they are comfortable. At some point if they have become successful enough, money will become secondary and sellers will not feel the need to work harder or longer.

A commission plan must reflect the company and management strategy and not simply pay people to sell things. Salespeople will operate as independent agents because that is what they are or that is what they have been told.

You can't tell a salesperson they are virtually in their own business and an independent agent if that is not true. You cannot treat sellers on commission like other employees on a guaranteed payroll.

Basing income on incentives or commissions *is incentive income.* The higher the commission and the less the guaranteed salary, the more independent a salesperson will operate. Sellers will try to earn up to their personal needs or motivation.

Salespeople will do what makes sense for their success and you can hardly blame them. It is not logical to work for less if you are capable of earning more.

It takes planning to set up sales pay plans to reach company goals and it is critically important to incentivize salespeople. Seller commission plans not structured correctly often result in a difficult sales force to manage and as well as create sales turnover.

The answer is not to figure out ways to pay sellers less than fair market income opportunities or you will be looking for increased sales turnover. Incentivize people properly for what you want accomplished.

What Men Can Learn From Women Sellers

Not only are women good at sales, they are often better or more active listeners. Women may be more likely to listen to problems and understand things before they have the urge to fix them. Listening skills lower ego problems and allows sellers to help accounts solve problems.

Women are perceptive at reading emotions and body language and may be likely to see the environment from a different perspective. They see things through their paradigms. Women in business are equally important consumers.

If you have women in your sales force, you must have women involved in thinking and planning. Women balance thinking and can see sales and marketing opportunities from a different perspective.

Selling is not a boys club. Women have sales instincts, mental capacity, drive, desire and determination as strong as men do and bring a needed dimension to a sales effort.

A woman is like a tea bag, you cannot tell how strong she is until you put her in hot water.

—**Nancy Reagan**

What Holds People Back

Daily operations and the finances of running a company or sales department can make people lose sight of an important fact. The manager's job is to shield sellers from time-consuming, non-productive activities. Managers must be creative, innovative and careful not to create down time for sellers. **Selling is a contact sport; sellers need to be in front of customers.**

Help Salespeople Help Themselves To Sell More

The more time with accounts and customers, the more sellers sell things. Sellers on average spend far too much time dealing with mistakes and problems. When customers do not get what is promised, they call the sellers. Most problems can be prevented with planning and foresight.

Companies cannot control competition or commodity pricing but they can control how well they use and support their salespeople.

Salespeople are the front line people and companies must capitalize on the valuable feedback of its sales force. Executive decisions coming from executive offices without input from the "street" may lead to uninformed decisions and assumptions.

In order to reach goals sales management must help sellers focus on revenue generating activities, provide training and give support. Sellers focus on what is measured.

Sales Managers Win When Sellers Are the Most Productive, *Not the Most Managed*

How You Think Is Everything

- Good Systems Drive Sales
- Interview To Find Strength
- Hire The 3 Ds: Drive-Determination-Desire
- Cut Losses Quickly And Move On
- Unproductive Sales Meetings Don't Lead To More Effective Selling
- Role-Play Is A Sure-Fire Solution To Sharpen Presenting Skills
- Sellers Don't Make A Good Collection Service
- Hire A Balanced Sales Force

Thanks For Reading!

I hope this book gives you sales ideas and incentive to create more success and have more fun. Times are extraordinary for good sellers as companies fight new battles in changing competitive markets. Sellers will become even more important in the future.

Companies are desperate for smart, creative, innovative salespeople. Keep a positive can-do attitude and don't stop learning new skills. Be extraordinary!

I wish you the best of luck and good selling.
Brian J. Bieler

Recommended Reading

Think and Grow Rich – Napoleon Hill

How to Win Friends and Influence People – Dale Carnegie

The Richest Man in Babylon – George S. Clason

The Art of War Sun Tzu – Translated by Thomas Cleary

Good to Great – Jim Collins

The 7 Habits of Highly Effective People – Stephen R. Covey

The Sales Bible – Jeffrey Gitomer

First, Break All the Rules – Marcus Buckingham

Spin Selling – Neil Rackman

Rich Dad, Poor Dad – Robert T. Kiyosaki

Who Moved My Cheese – Spencer Johnson, M.D.

The Tipping Point – Malcolm Gladwell

Revolutionary Wealth – Alvin & Heidi Toffler

Leadership Secrets of Attila the Hun – Wess Roberts

The 22 Immutable Laws of Marketing – Al Ries & Jack Trout

How to Present Like a Pro – Lani Arredondo

The One Minute Manager – Kenneth H. Blanchard

About The Author

Brian J. Bieler

Brian J. Bieler has more than thirty plus years of business, managing, marketing and sales experience. He began his career selling copy paper and by the age of twenty-four was a sales supervisor in midtown Manhattan.

Brian then went into the advertising business at *Women's Wear Daily* and *Mademoiselle Magazine* in New York City. Later he joined Sudbrink Broadcasting, a leading-edge radio group specializing in buying and improving underperforming companies.

He was Vice President and General Manager of ten major market radio stations from coast to coast and President of the Viacom Radio Group in New York City. He produced workshops with Excellerated Business Schools and was President of WestWorks Marketing.

To Order Books

Telephone Orders: 1-800-980-5099

Email Book Orders or contact: powerfulsteps@cox.net

Postal Orders:
Little Falls Press
7000 North 16th Street, Suite 120 #489
Phoenix, AZ, 85020

Please send (number of copies_____) The Sales Operator to:

Name (please print):_____

Address:_____

City:_____State:_____Zip:_____

Country:_____

Telephone:_____

Email address:_____

$17.95 U.S. Dollars per book.

Arizona residents please add local sales tax.

U. S. Shipping and Handling add $4.00 per book and $2.00 for each additional book in same shipment.

International Shipping and handling add $8.00 per book and $5.00 for each additional book in same shipment.

Payment: Cheque: ☐   Credit Card: ☐

Visa:☐ Master Card:☐ AMEX:☐ Discover:☐

Card Number:_____

Name On Card:_____

Expiration Date On Card:_____

**Visit our web site
www.powerfulsteps.com**

www.ingramcontent.com/pod-product-compliance
Lightning Source LLC
Chambersburg PA
CBHW031932190326
41519CB00007B/503